SEWING FOR SUCCESS
AN ILLUSTRATED GUIDE FOR BEGINNERS

Michele Bledsoe

BOOK BOOK²

Book Book Squared
P.O. Box 60144
Colorado Springs, Colorado
80960

✺

Published in the United States of America by
Book Book Squared
P.O. Box 60144
Colorado Springs, Colorado 80960

Sewing for Success
An Illustrated Guide for Beginners

Michele Bledsoe

1st edition: January 1, 2024

ISBN: 978-1-943829-49-1

✺

Book design/layout - Donald Kallaus
Photography and Illustrations by Michele Bledsoe
Book Book Squared is an imprint of Rhyolite Press LLC

To my Grandmother, and cousins–Betty and Patty

When I was born my grandmother lived with us and was the first person to hold me when I came home from the hospital. Soon after, she went out and bought a new 1953 sewing machine. With this machine she taught me to sew. Not long after I finished college for Fashion, she passed away, and I inherited the machine.

I have now been sewing since age seven; sewing has been my therapy and my passion.

TABLE OF CONTENTS

INTRODUCTION

Being from an older generation, I learned to sew, as many women did, from older family members. Starting at the age of seven, sewing became a passion for me. Making things for others as well as myself has been very fulfilling. Today, sewing is a disappearing life skill. Sewing is like putting together a puzzle with the feeling of accomplishment when the job is completed. Constructing a puzzle without a clear picture of the end result would be difficult.

It is my hope that this book will help teach the young, as well as adults, the joy of sewing and give them a clear picture of how to plan for success. It touches on the basics needed to understand terms used in sewing. It is an introduction to the parts and functions of a sewing machine, what type of fabric is best suited for a project, what supplies should be on hand prior to starting, how to read a pattern, and so much more. I hope this informational guide will help you on the road to Sewing Success!

Michele Bledsoe

SEWING FOR SUCCESS

AN ILLUSTRATED GUIDE FOR BEGINNERS

PART ONE

*What's Needed To Know
Before You Sew*

Parts of the Sewing Machine ———

It is important to know what type of sewing machine will best fit your needs in learning how to sew. A sewing machine with many functions and computerized chips is wonderful for an experienced person, but a basic sewing machine will be less confusing to learn on and be a better investment for a beginner. A sewing machine with high-end computer chips can be expensive to fix and most functions are not necessary when one is learning.

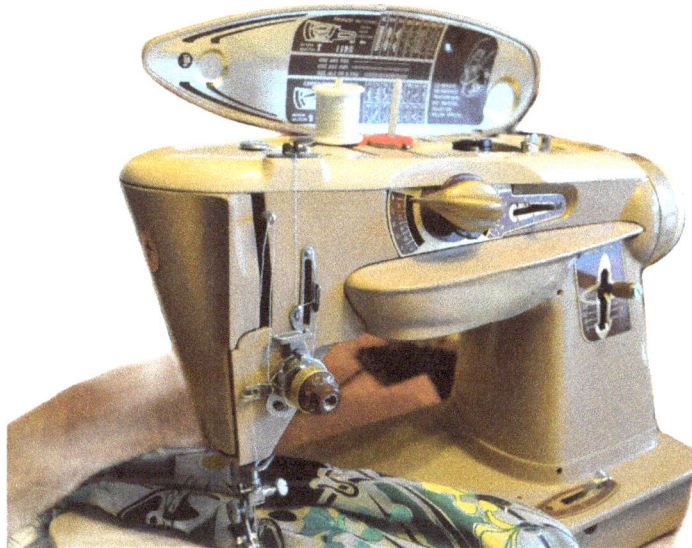

Figure 1-1

There are many parts to a sewing machine that will be covered in later sections of this book. The following are the main parts that need to be understood to begin sewing.

Manual

Make sure that you have the manual for your sewing machine. If no manual came with your machine, in the case of a used or older machine, most manuals can be found on the internet. Search for a manual using the make of your sewing machine and serial number. This information is usually found on the front or underneath your machine. The manual will describe the following parts of your sewing machine as described below.

Reverse Button

The Reverse Button (or lever) will allow the machine to go forward or in reverse. When starting a straight stitch, it is best to go forward, then backward, then forward again so that the thread is held in place. It is best to go one-quarter of an inch forward, then back over those stitches, then forward again to secure the thread so the garment does not pull apart. This is called backstitching that will be covered later in more detail you may find different types of reverse buttons.

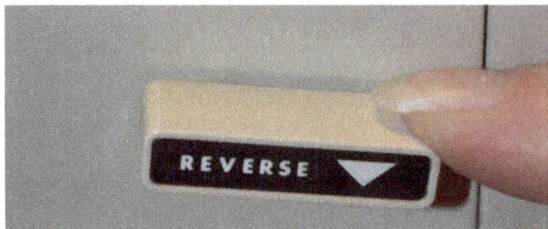
Figure 1-2

Thread Locations

When using a sewing machine, thread is located in two parts of the machine, one on the top (in the main spool of thread) and one in a compartment under the needle (in a bobbin). The two threads are then bound together with each stitch.

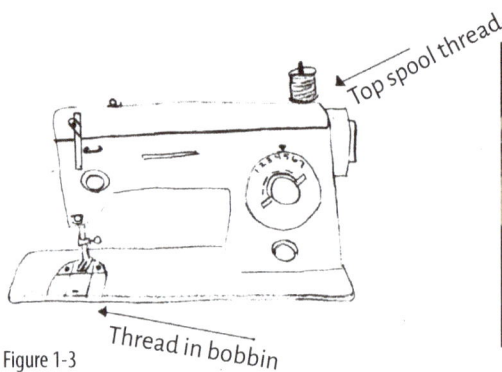
Figure 1-3

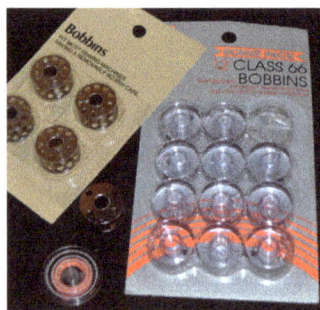
Figure 1-4 Bobbins

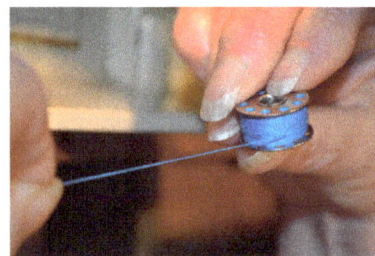
Figure 1-5

Bobbin

A bobbin is a round disc usually made of plastic or metal. Most new machines come with multiple bobbins. Having several are useful for different thread colors. Having several bobbins saves time for not having to unthread your machine to wind a new bobbin. Although there are generic bobbins that are made to fit in most sewing machines, it is best to use bobbins that are a match for your machine. To ensure you buy the correct bobbins for your machine, bring a bobbin that came with your machine to a fabric store. The back of the bobbin package will show what make of sewing machine they will fit.

Figure 1-6

Figure 1-7

Bobbins do not hold as much thread as a spool, so plan ahead. Winding two bobbins in the needed thread color for your project will save time. Refer to your manual for the process to wind a bobbin with thread.

Figure 1-8

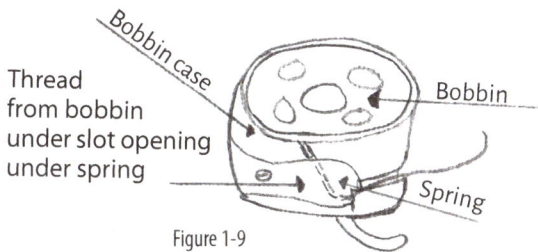

Thread
from bobbin
under slot opening
under spring

Bobbin case

Bobbin

Spring

Figure 1-9

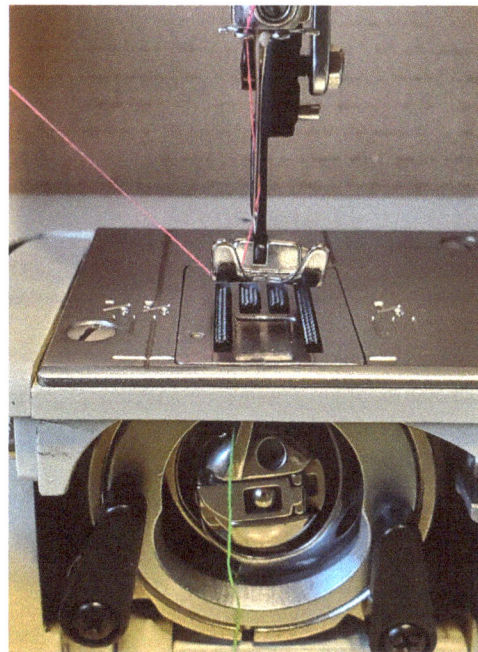

Figure 1-10

Pattern Selection Button

Not all sewing machines have this button but most do. If your sewing machine has this button, it is used to choose the type of seam needed: a straight stitch seam or a seam that has a zigzag. A zigzag is used for buttonholes and as a securing stitch for fabrics than can unravel. For beginners, only two stitches are needed, the straight stitch and the zigzag stitch. The zigzag stitch is probably the second most common stitch you will be using. More advanced sewing machines can create fancier stitches and do embroidery all by a computer chip. Sewing machines in the past have pattern cams, which can do more stitches than zigzag.

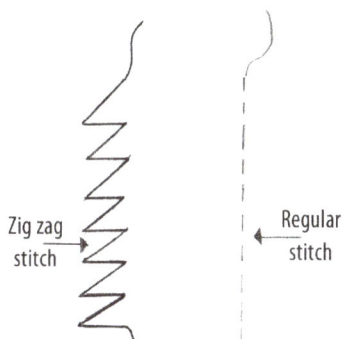

Zig zag
stitch

Regular
stitch

Figure 1-11 Zig zag vs regular stitch

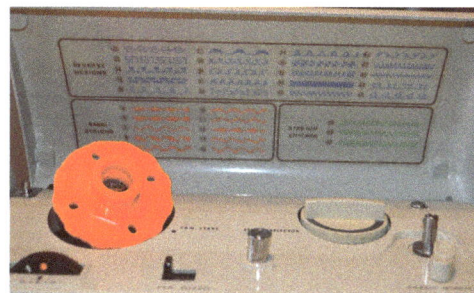

Figure 1-12 Pattern Cam

Straight Stitch Dial

This dial determines how many stitches per inch will be sewn. The smaller the number the

Figure 1-13

more stitches per inch. Often patterns will tell you to baste parts of the fabric to gather or hold fabric in place (not a permanent stitch but a temporary long loose stitch used for preparation). Gathering is used on a sleeve or around a waistband. When gathering a fabric, you want a very loose stitch so it is easy to remove. This dial also controls the tension for the thread spool on top of your sewing machine (figure 1-14).

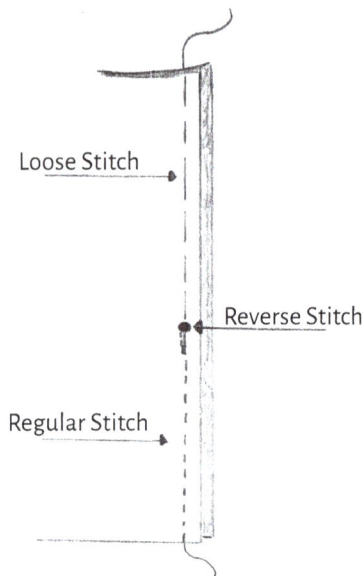

Figure 1-14

This dial is the only one you need to frequently adjust for the length of a stitch and the length for basting. If your stitch is too small, the stitches will be too close together and will gather, puckering the fabric. The machine will then have problems moving forward. If you set it for too long of a stitch, the stitches will pull apart under pressure.

Thread Take-Up Lever

This lever is important when you are considering buying a sewing machine or if you already have one. It looks like a little hook that comes out with a hole at the top. It is on the top part of the sewing machine. It goes up and down when your machine is sewing and looks like an arm that comes up with a hole in it that your thread goes through when you are threading your machine. The importance of this lever is to remember that if it is not a closed hole, the thread can slip off the back of the arm and your machine will jam up and stop sewing. If it has a closed hole, the thread will not come off while sewing. It is best to have a machine that has the little hook with a closed hole rather than a wedge that your thread can slip off.

Figure 1-15 Take-up lever

Tension Adjuster

Some older sewing machines will have a small dial on the front that sticks out and has several numbers with a negative and positive sign on it. This is a

Figure 1-16 Tension Bobbin

tension adjuster. This dial should not be adjusted if the sewing machine is sewing properly. This tension dial is for the bobbin which is used for different weights of fabrics. Most of the time this dial is set to handle the average fabric weight. Once adjusted, it is hard to adjust back to where it needs to be. The only tension dial you need to adjust is the one for the thread spool number on the top of the dial (figure 1-18). You will not need to adjust the bobbin tension for fabric that is two layers thick; will need the right needle size for the type of fabric.

Figure 1-17 Tension Bobbin

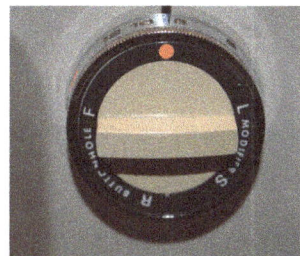

Figure 1-18

Presser Foot

This attachment holds fabric in place when sewing. Underneath the presser foot is a throat plate that has "Feed dogs" which are

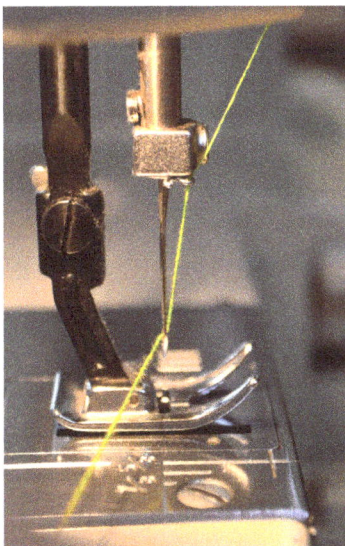

Figure 1-20 Presser Foot

jagged bars that move back-and-forth. The feed dogs (figure 1-21) move the fabric through the machine. They hold fabric between foot and throat plate so it will sew and move smoothly forward and backwards. Beginners often want to pull fabric through, but the presser foot and feed dogs will do that at the proper speed. Pulling fabric through will bend the needle and possibly break it. The presser foot lever is down

Figure 1-19

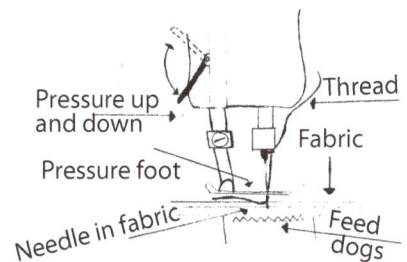

Figure 1-21 Feed dogs

when sewing and up when taking fabric out or placing fabric in the sewing machine. "Sewing machine feed dogs are metal teeth-like ridges that emerge from a hole in the *throat plate* of a sewing machine. Feed dogs move as you sew, gently gripping the bottom fabric to help it pass through the sewing machine and produce a high-quality stitch. The plate under the presser foot, where the feed dogs are, is called the *throat plate*."

Figure 1-22 Presser foot - down

Figure 1-23 Presser foot - up

Seam Allowance Guide

The numbers going across to the right or to the left on the throat plate are a sewing guide. They help guide you to make a straight seam. Most garments use a 5/8" seam. The guide will also have other numbers that a pattern might require. If using an older machine that does not have such a guide, mark a 5/8" measure to the right from where the needle goes down into the fabric.

Tape a piece of paper with a 5/8" mark on your machine next to the needle position to use as a seam guide. Beginners tend to look at the needle when sewing, but to make straight seams, it is best to use the allowance guide.

Sewing Light

This is part of the sewing machine to help see better close up. The light can be found under the neck or on the left side (next page). The light bulb should pop out or unscrew, but check your machine's manual.

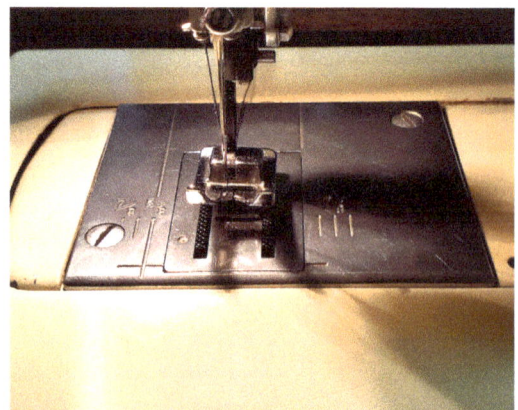

Figure 1-24 Seam Allowance "Measure" Guide

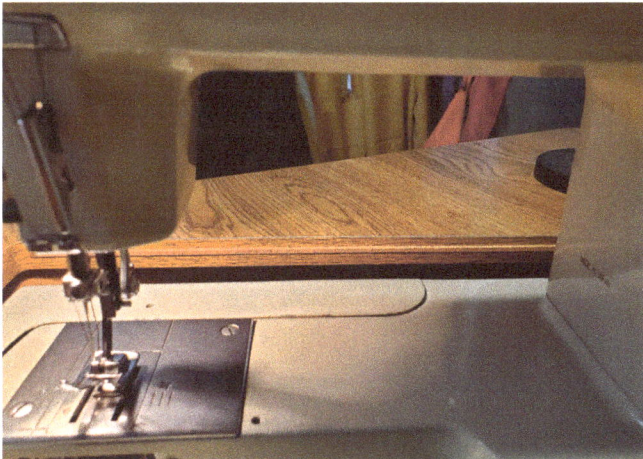

Figure 1-25 Light under the machine neck

Figure 1-26 sewing light

Hand Wheel

The hand wheel is usually on the right side of your sewing machine because most people are

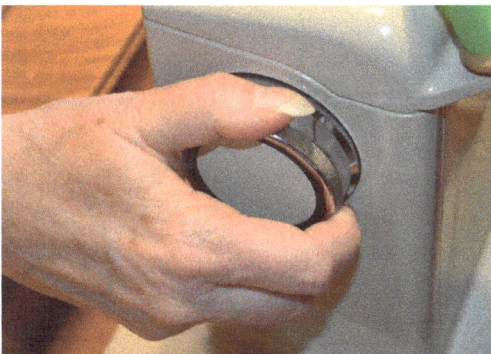

Figure 1-27 Hand wheel

right handed. It turns when the foot control is in use or can be operated by hand by turning it towards you. It will make the needle go up and down instead of using the foot control.

Often, when finished with a seam, the machine has not released the fabric because the needle has not completed its rotation. To complete the rotation, turn the hand wheel towards you to release the thread. The fabric should then pull easily from your machine. If needed, turn the hand wheel to cut your threads and start your next stitch. Leave a few inches of thread going through the needle and from the bobbin. If there is not enough thread to start to sew, the needle will become unthreaded (figure 1-28).

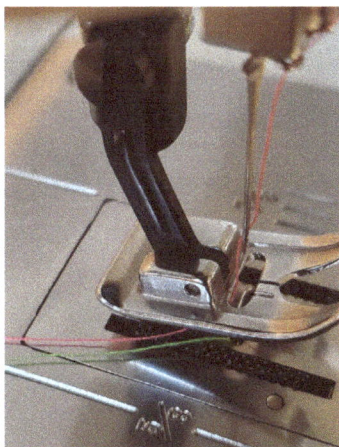

Figure 1-28 Unthreaded needle

On/Off Switch – Safety Hint

If you have children around, you do not want to leave the machine on. If the light is off and the machine is not operating you may think that the machine is off, but it still can be "on."

To test your machine, make sure that when the foot pedal is pushed down it does not operate. No child should be allowed to play with your sewing machine without supervision. It is especially dangerous for a child to place their hand under the needle. Know where the turn-off switch is located and make sure that your machine is unplugged. The turn-on or off switch can be found on the right hand side of the sewing machine. If you have children around, use nail polish to mark the dials to the proper settings. If someone then changes the dial settings, you can easily move them to the correct settings.

Before starting to sew, you need to gather the necessary sewing supplies. Sewing supplies are known as notions. Below is a standard supply list.

Notions and Accessories ———

1. Sewing Machine
2. Sewing Machine Bobbins
3. Seam Ripper
4. Hand Sewing Needles
5. Sewing Machine Needles
6. Pins (small glass-ball headed)
7. Dressmaker's Shears
8. No. 2 Pencil (soft lead)
9. Dressmaker's Chalk Pencil
10. Tape Measure and Yardstick
11. Thread
12. Zipper Foot and/or Buttonhole Foot (as needed for your project)

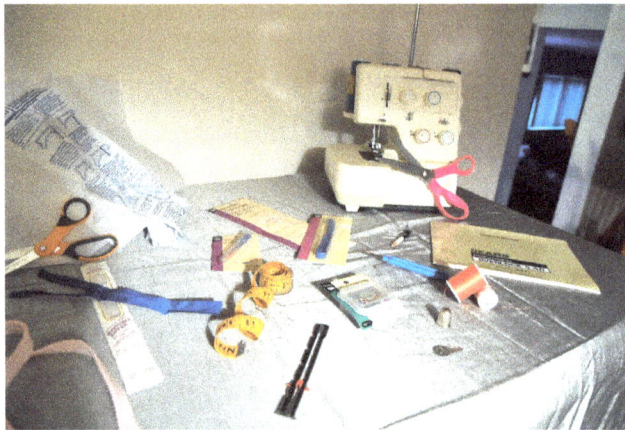

Figure 1-29 The things you'll need

Figure 1-30

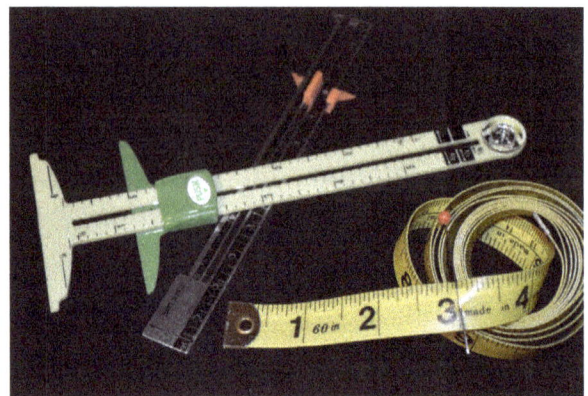

Figure 1-31 Items for measuring

Standard accessories that come with your sewing machine are bobbins and a seam ripper (figure 1-32). A seam ripper is used for taking out seams that have been incorrectly sewn. The

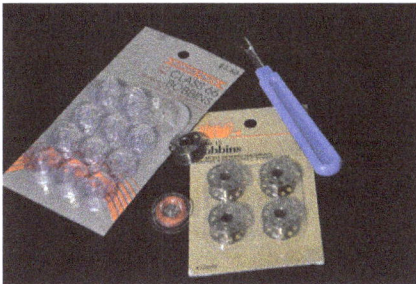

new machines will come with these or they can be purchased in any sewing department. A seam ripper can easily take out seam mistakes.

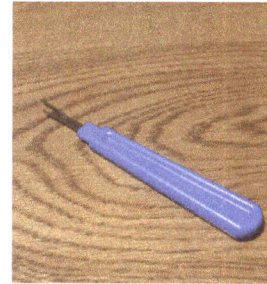

Figure 1-32 Bobbins

Figure 1-33 Seam Ripper

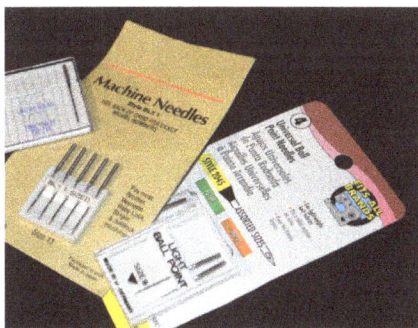

Both standard hand sewing needles and replacement sewing machine needles should be kept in supply. There are two different types of sewing machine needles. The "standard" needles that will sew all fabrics excluding stretch knits (tee-shirt or swimwear) and the "ball-point" needles

Figure 1-34 Machine Needles

used for knit fabric. The ball-point needle is a bit rounded at the end. It goes in and out of the fabric without breaking

the thread of the fabric. When a thread is broken, knit fabrics unravel or it makes a hole, like a nylon stocking (figure 1-35). The type of needle required for certain types of fabrics will be discussed in later chapters.

Packets of both types of needles can be purchased for hand or sewing machines at all fabric stores. The back of needle packets will specify which needles are used for various sewing machines and for which weights of fabrics they are appropriate.

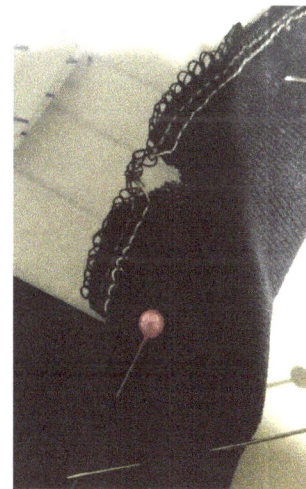

Figure 1-35

There are different types of straight pins. Ball-headed pins are used to hold the fabric and the pattern pieces together when laying out the pattern and for pinning sections of a garment in place to sew or cut out. Some have colored balls on the end and some are glass. Choose which are easiest for you to use. Some pins are magnetized. If you drop magnetized pins, a magnet can

Figure 1-36 Sewing Pins

quickly pick them up, but magnets can cause problems near computerized sewing machines. For knits, use ball-headed pins as they are rounded on the end.

Sharp scissors and pinking shears are necessities when sewing. Pinking shears are scissors with blades that are serrated instead of straight. They leave a zigzag cut rather than a straightedge cut. These are recommended when using fabrics that unravel. Sharp scissors, designated for fabric use, will make it easier when cutting out a pattern, when your garment is washed, the edge that is pinking sheared will not ball up and will not unravel.

Chalk pencils or tailors chalk are used for marking patterns on fabric and will wash out.

Tape measures will be used for various needs in sewing. A handy measure is a hem ruler which has a slide to one side to make the bottom of the hem even.

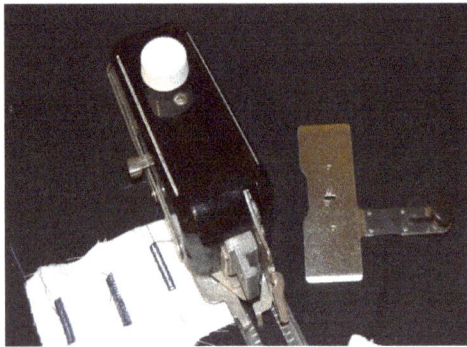

Figure 1-37 Button Hole Maker

There are several different buttonhole feet. Some look like little slide rules; those are for newer sewing machines. Other ones have a bar that interchanges with the pressure foot (figure 1-37).

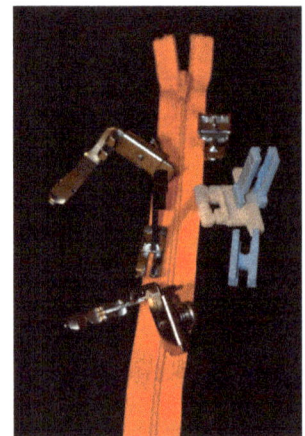

Figure 1-38 Zipper foot

A zipper foot replaces the presser foot when sewing a zipper (figure1-38).

The use of different feet will be further discussed later in the book.

Threading and Practice Stitching ———

Now that you are a bit more familiar with your machine, let's get started learning how to sew. You are not going to start sewing on a garment yet. You are going to sew on fabric and make some stitches. This will help you to be more comfortable with your sewing machine. First you need to thread the sewing machine and bobbin. Start by placing your thread spool on the

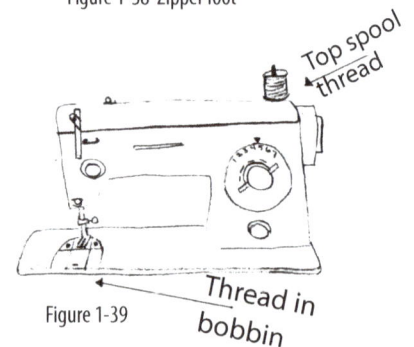

Figure 1-39

Top spool thread

Thread in bobbin

stem on top of the machine (figure 1-39). To thread your machine, refer to your manual as all machines are different. You can also look online for illustrations of how to thread your machine using its model number.

Next wind the bobbin. Do not wind the bobbin so full that it will be tight in the bobbin casing (follow figures 1-40 through 1-49). Finally you will draw thread from the bobbin up through the throat plate (follow figures 1-50 through 1-55).

Figure 1-40

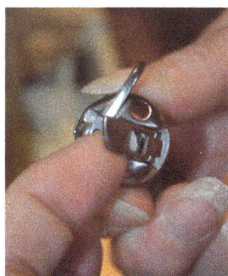

Figure 1-41

Figure 1-42

Figure 1-43

Figure 1-44

Figure 1-45

Figure 1-46

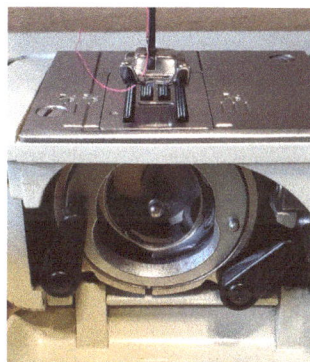

Figure 1-47

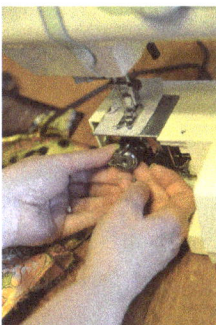

Figure 1-48

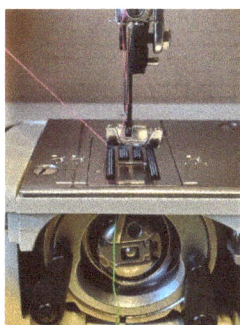

Figure 1-49

Figure 1-50

Figure 1-51

Figure 1-52

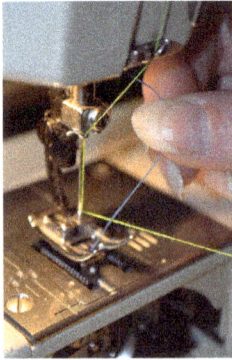
Figure 1-53

Figure 1-54

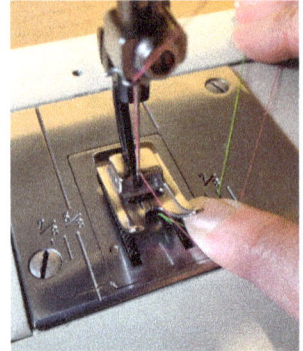
Figure 1-55

You will now begin sewing on a piece of fabric or interfacing (fabric added to stiffen a garment piece). Note: Never sew on just a piece of tissue paper (used in making patterns) without fabric underneath. That will jam up your machine. Always be sewing on some type of fabric.

On a piece of fabric, draw a straight line with a pencil; then draw a curved line; then draw a square box (figure 1-56). To secure the fabric underneath the presser foot, lift the lever on the back of the machine (figure 0026 A, 0026), slide the fabric under the presser foot, then lower the lever to secure the fabric before beginning to sew (figures 1-57 & 1-58). The presser foot will hold the fabric so it won't slide when sewing forward or when using the reverse button to go backward (figure 1-60).

Figure 1-56

Figure 1-57

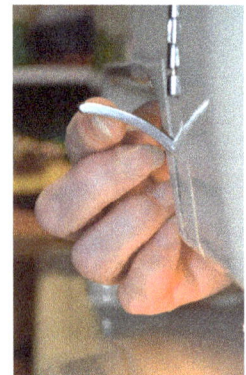
Figure 1-58

Figure 1-59

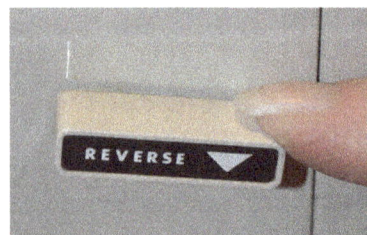
Figure 1-60

Start sewing forward on the straight line. *It may take a little time for you find the right speed when sewing Use your knee or the foot pedal to experiment until you are comfortable finding the right speed. The picture of the Parts of the Sewing Machine Cabinet in your manual is where to find how to use the knee control or the foot pedal (will be placed on the floor) (figure 1-61) Sew forward a couple inches, stop, and then use the reverse button to go backward. Then stop and go forward. Keep alternating between a few

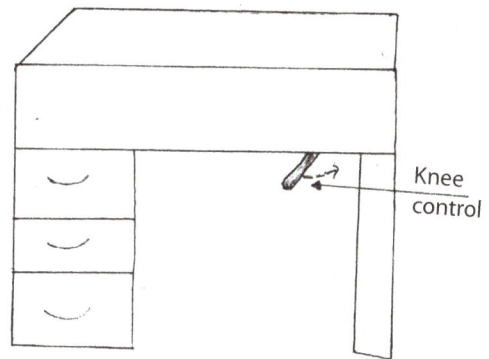

Figure 1-61   Sewing cabinet

inches in each direction until you can do so while keeping your stitches on the line. When you move your hand side-to-side as the fabric slides, do not push the fabric. The feed dogs in the throat plate underneath the fabric will move the fabric along at the correct speed.

After you have finished the straight line, try the curved line, sewing at a moderate speed. Using both hands, gently turn the fabric to follow the curve as the feed dogs move it forward (figure 1-59).

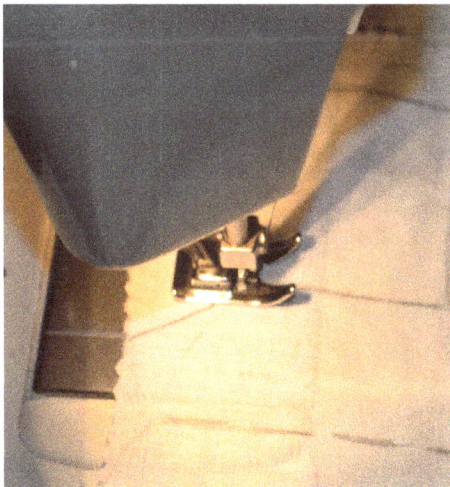

Figure 1-62 Sewing the box

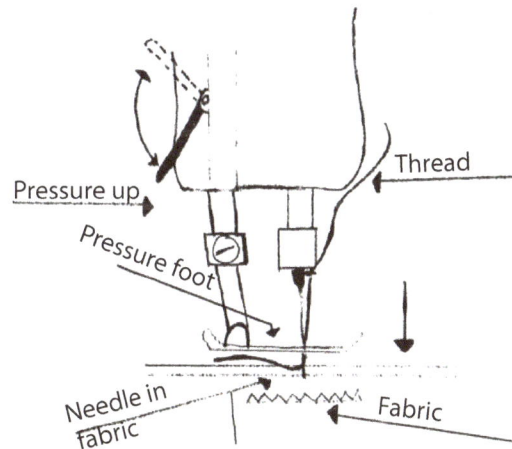

Figure 1-63

Next is the box (figure 1-62). When sewing a box, stitch along one side of the box until you come to the corner. At the corner, stop stitching leaving the needle down through the fabric (figure 1-63). Lift up the presser foot (figure 1-58, opposite), rotate your fabric a quarter-turn, and then lower the presser foot (figure 1-57, opposite) so that you are facing the next side of the box. Continue around the box until you come to your starting point.

If you have trouble with any sewing tasks, feel free to ask for help at any fabric store.

Measuring and Understanding Pattern Sizes —————— Sizes of patterns can be confusing to those beginning to sew. A pattern size does NOT correlate to the size of an item in the store. To sell clothing, stores use smaller size numbers to entice the shopper to purchase more. Size for a pattern must be found through measurements.

Three measurements are what you will need for most patterns.
Start at the top using a cloth tape measure.

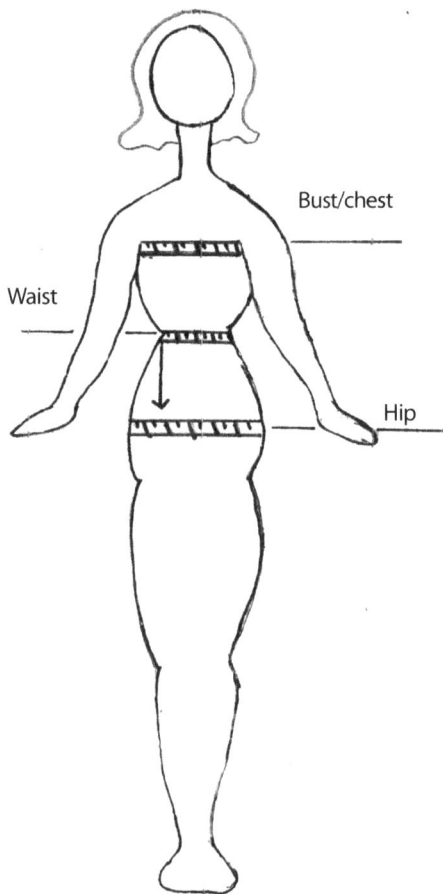

Figure 1-64

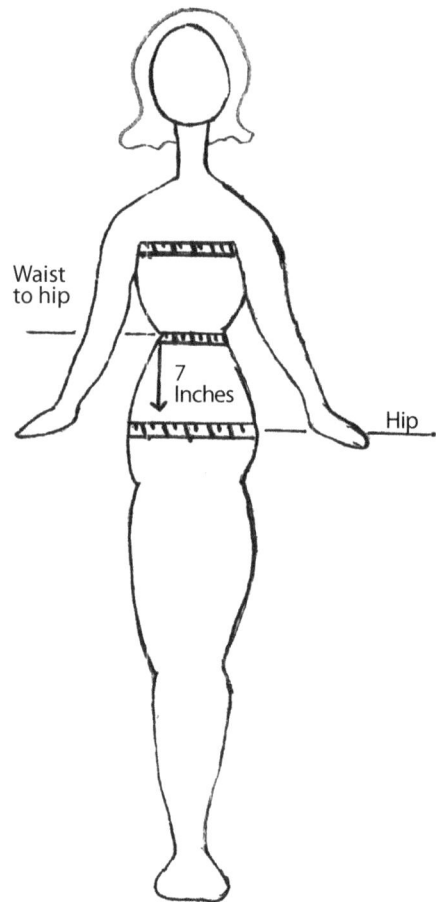

Figure 1-65

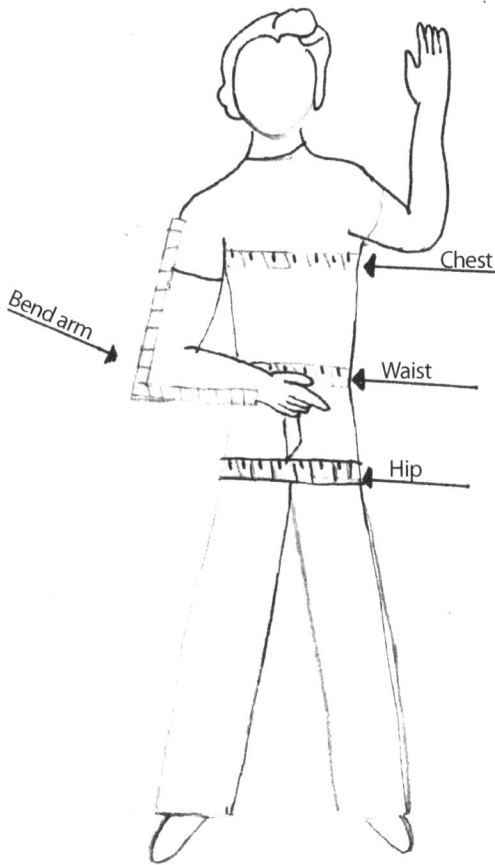

Bust/Chest, measure under arms_____

Waist_____

Hips, always measure 7" down from the waist_____

To measure hips, put the tape measure at the waist, then measure down 7" on each side of the hips and mark those points with pins or a chalk mark. Use the tape measure around the hips at those points to find the hip measurement (figure 1-65).

Children's sizes can be by age or measurements. If they are six years old, they will normally take a size 6.

Patterns differ by designer or manufacturer (McCalls, Butterick, Simplicity, etc.). Do not focus on the size number; go by your measurements for the best fit.

Figure 1-66

When sewing for a man, McCall's patterns measure differently for sleeves. Measuring the arm with a slight bend gives a more natural measurement. Measure from top of the arm, over bent elbow, to wrist.

Shopping for and Understanding Patterns ————

The following "Pattern Field Trip" will take about two hours at a fabric store. This will familiarize you with how to find what you want at a fabric store, the different kinds of notions and accessories they have, and where to find patterns.

Author's Note:
This can be fun if going with a friend or relative. I used to do this with my daughter and we both enjoyed the experience.

To take the Pattern Field Trip, go to the Pattern Area of the store:

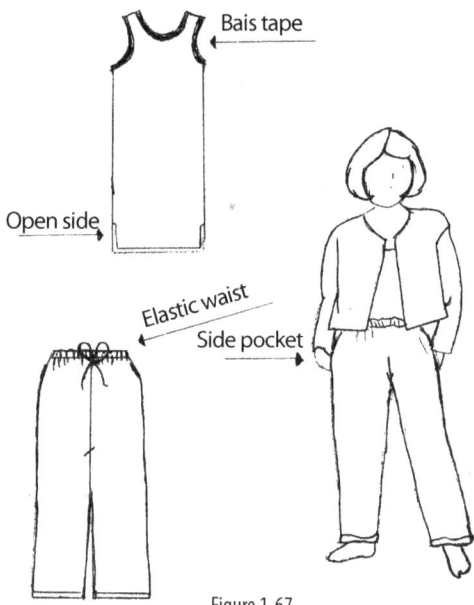

Figure 1-67

- Pattern Books – *Be sure to bring your measurements. Find the pattern sections best for you—children's, women's, men's, costumes, plus-sizes, pajamas, etc. Look at patterns for various types of garments. Be sure to check several from each of the various designers or manufacturer (McCalls, Butterick, Simplicity, etc.) Focus on the style of the garment, not what fabric the pictures show.

Things to consider:

- Does it have a waistline?

- What kind of sleeves?

- Collars: button-down, V-neck, pull-over, etc.

- Does it have a neckband, cuffs, zippers, etc?

- Does it have a jacket?

- Does it have pockets? (figure 1-67)

- Dresses with or without darts? (figure 1-69)
   *Often preferred for busty persons so the garment will hang properly. (figure 1-68)

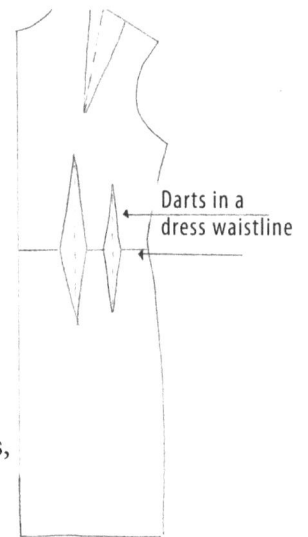

Figure 1-69

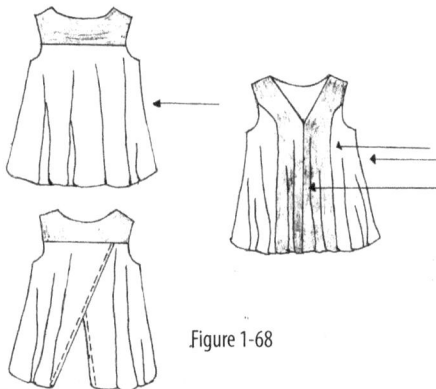

Figure 1-68

Using a Pattern Book - *Many are also written in Spanish or French

- Check the colored tabs on the side which is the index to find what you want: dresses, tops, vests, jackets, sportswear, junior sizes, children's sizes, unisex (appropriate for a woman or a man), craft items, costumes, etc.

- Patterns will have a photo or drawing showing different views. At the bottom of the picture, it will have a pencil drawing of what it looks like from the back of the garment. This is where you can tell if there are darts, pockets, etc.

- Look for elastic wrists or waistlines, slits on the side, dropped sleeves, etc.

Finding and Using a Pattern
*You will look these up in the book, then find them in the pattern drawers.

- The pattern number is at the very top, such as 8686.

- The envelope will indicate what sizes are available for each pattern.(picture 033)

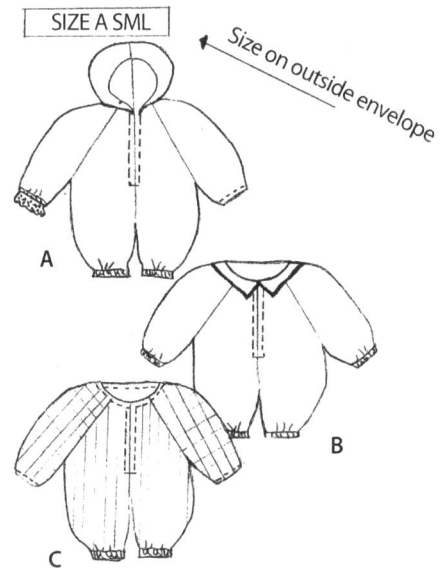

Figure 1-70

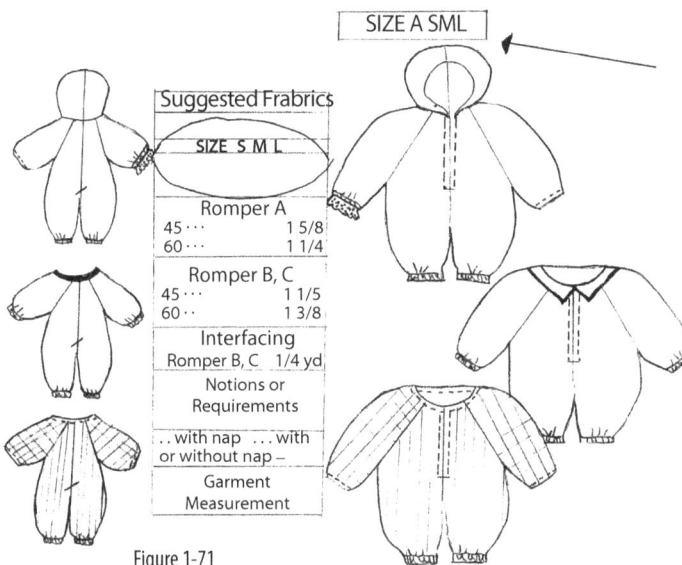

Figure 1-71

- A size such as K may indicate that this pattern can be used for sizes 8, 10, 12; M may indicate it can be used for sizes 14, 16, 18; Z may indicate it can be used for sizes 20, 22, 26; etc.

- Be sure the pattern you are buying is correct for *your* measurement size (see figure 1-71).

- Check the back of the envelope for measurement information (see figure 1-72, next page).

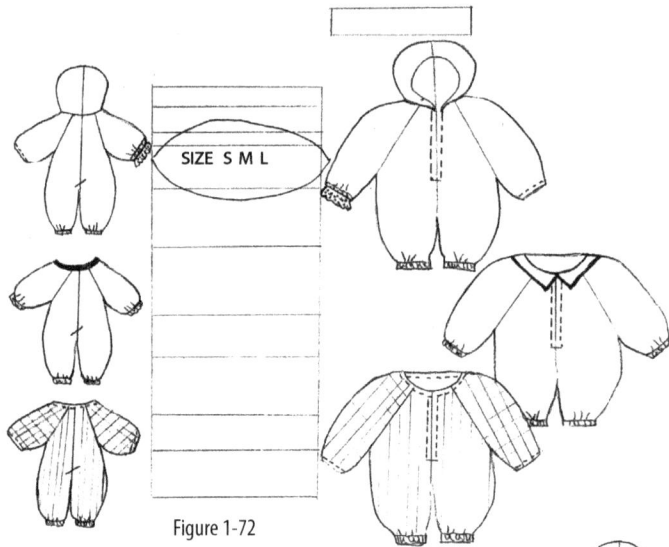

Figure 1-72

- If the measurements are an inch off, it may be loose-fitting; then do not go to the bigger size, especially if the garment has an elastic waist.

- If you are in-between sizes, choose the larger size as it is easier to make it smaller for you.

- Read all the information on the back of the pattern.

- Some patterns will suggest what fabrics are best for the garment (figure 1-73), notions recommended thread, elastic, buttons, etc. (figure 1-74), if lining or interfacing are required (figure 1-75) etc.

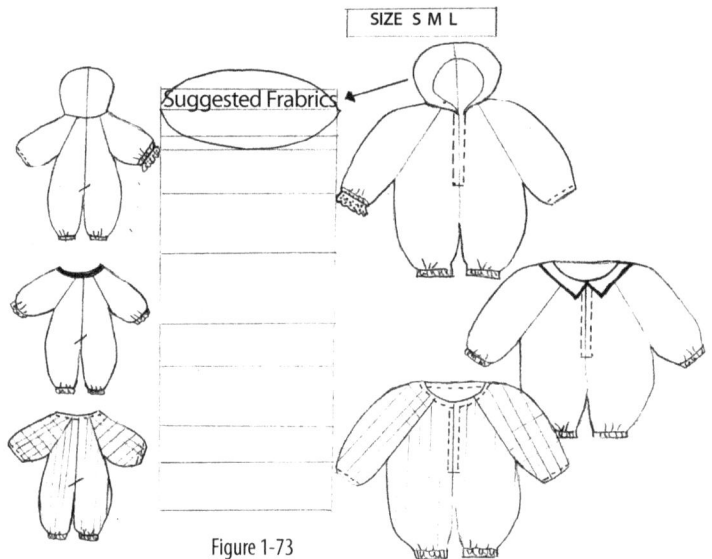

SIZE S M L

Suggested Frabrics

Figure 1-73

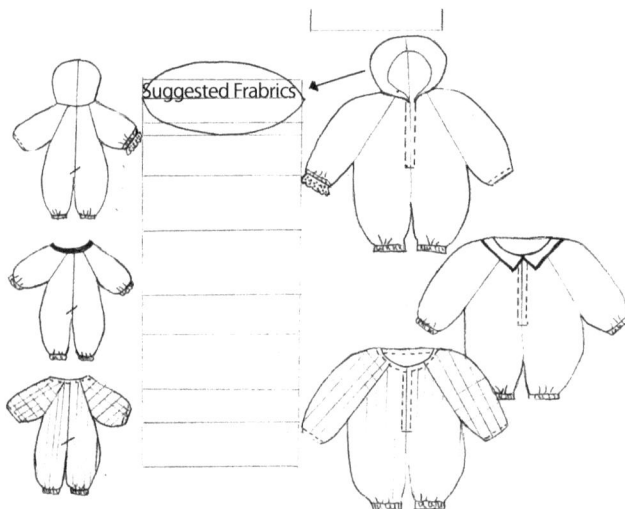

Suggested Frabrics

Figure 1-74

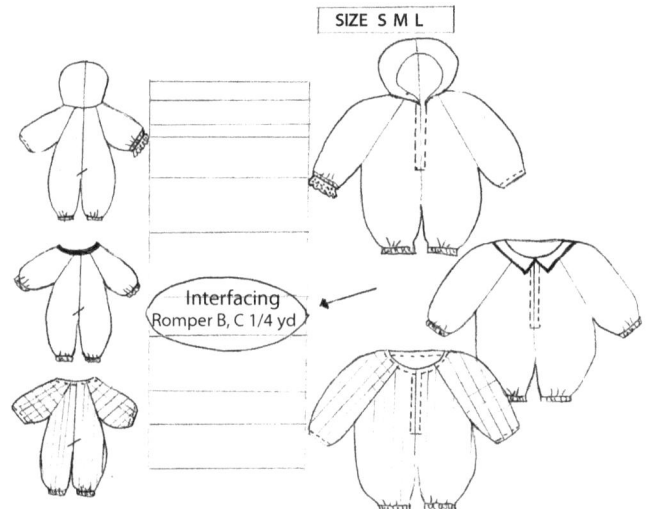

SIZE S M L

Interfacing
Romper B, C 1/4 yd

Figure 1-75

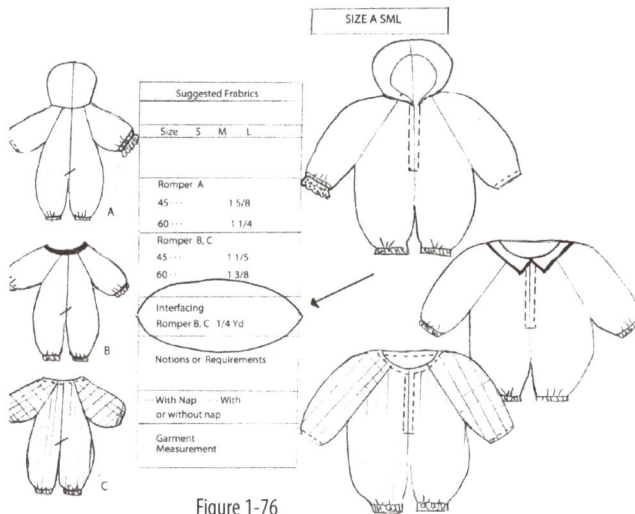

Figure 1-76

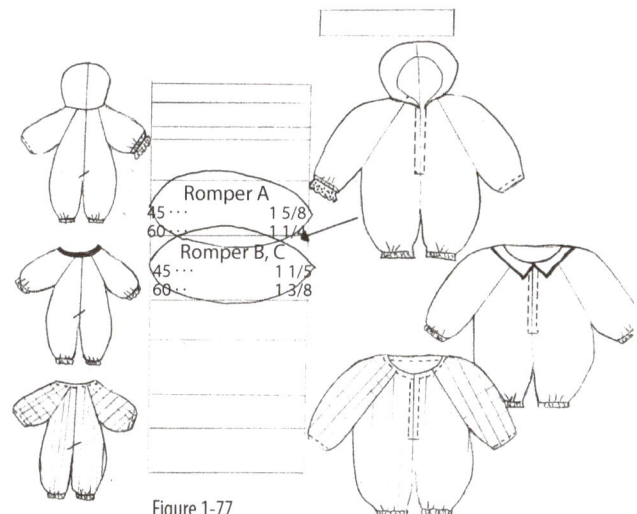

Figure 1-77

- Patterns often tell if the garment is loose-fitting or if it has a yoke. A yoke means that it is fitted. Most men have yokes on their shirts, which means that the shirt has two pieces, one that goes over the shoulder.

- Jacket or pants patterns may say fit or semi-fitted.

- Under the column for your size on the back of the envelope, you can find the fabric width, 45 width or 60 width, which is the width in inches of the fabric you need to purchase (figure 1-77).

As always, ask a salesperson if you have questions.

A serger is a special type of sewing machine that finishes off seam edges, but most beginning sewers would just use a pinking shears for this purpose.

Patterns and Notions ———

Sewing supplies are known as notions that are used to make professional, finished garments.

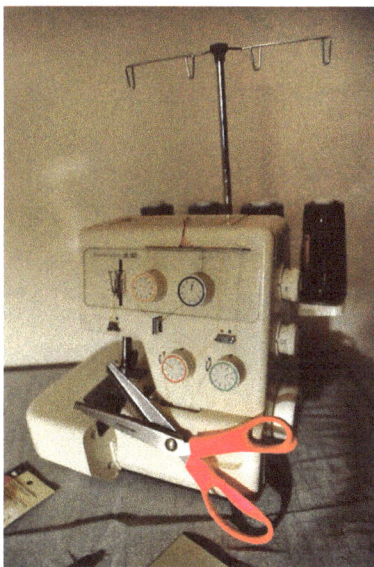

Figure 1-78 Serger sewing machine

Notions and Their Uses:

● Pinking Shears –These are scissors that have jagged edges. They are used to cut fabric so the threads do not unravel (top, figure 1-79)

● Ball-point Sewing Needles – These are used for the same purpose as ball-point pins see figure 1-80). They are used for knitted fabrics that can unravel, like a tee-shirt or a woven fabric, which have interlocking threads. One thread can unravel the whole garment, similar to a knit sweater with a hole in it (figure 1-81). When sewing knitted fabrics, you do not want to break the threads or your garment will end up with holes in it instead of broken stitches. Ball-point needles are rounded on the end and separate the threads in your fabric instead of breaking them. *For non-knit fabrics such as cottons, use straight pins and needles.

Figure 1-79 Pinking Shears, top of picture

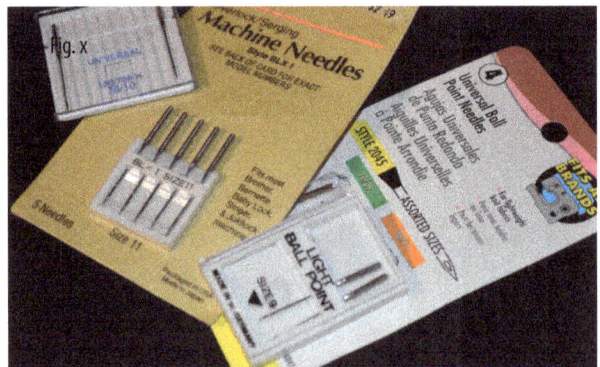

Figure 1-80 Machine Needles and Ball-point needles

● Scissors – Scissors are made in both right-handed orientation and left-handed orientation. Do NOT use sewing scissors to cut paper or anything else. They should only be used for fabric. You may want to put a ribbon on the handle or mark it with nail polish.

Author's Note:
My husband once used my sewing scissors to cut wire. Once they have been used to cut something else, they no longer work well on fabric. If your sewing scissors need sharpening, take them to a fabric store or somewhere that sharpens knives.

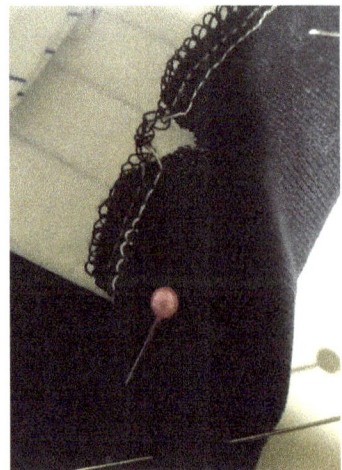

Figure 1-81

Figure 1-82

● Thread – Take your fabric to a fabric store to match your thread to your fabric. At the top of a spool of thread, you should be able to unhook the end of the thread from a notch in the spool base to lay that thread against your fabric to see if it matches. Hold up several spools of thread near your fabric until you find the one that is the best match. There should be little to no difference in the colors. Top of the spool of thread is colored for different types of thread. Cotton, Silk, Heavy Duty and All Purpose. You will be using All-Purpose thread as it has polyester in it so will not shrink when washed.

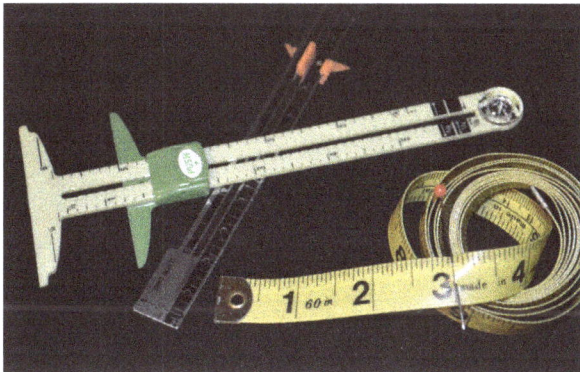

Figure 1-83 Sewing guage and measuring tape

● Cloth Tape Measure – These roll up and are easy to use for finding body measurements.

● Sewing Gauge – This is typically a 6-inch metal scale, marked in both inches and centimeters, with a sliding pointer. It is most often used to measure and mark hem or seam allowances, button placement, button sizes, tucks, and pleats.

● Seam Ripper – This is a valuable tool that makes taking out incorrect stitches easy and, when carefully used, does not damage the fabric.

● A Regular Soft Lead No. 2 Pencil – The softer lead can be used for marking fabrics and the marks easily wash out. You can also use a white pencil from a colored pencil set. These are most useful when marking dark-colored fabric.

Types of Fabric _____

Be sure to use the right fabric for your sewing project (figure 1-85). The backs of pattern envelopes give

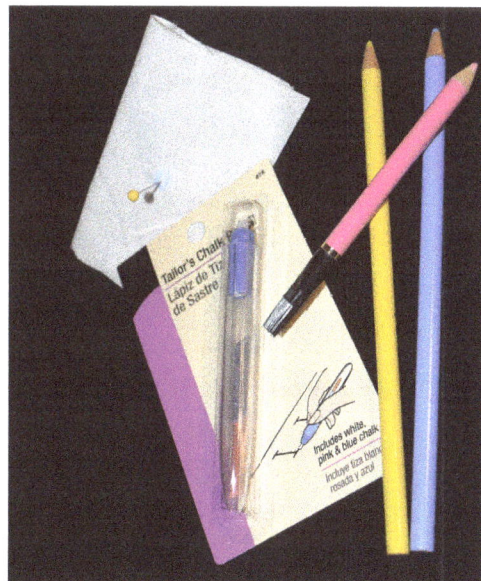

Figure 1-84 Marking Pencils

recommendations for fabrics most suitable for that garment. Also given are the possible fabric widths most appropriate for your project and how much fabric should be used. Most fabrics are either 45" or 60" wide (figure 1-86).

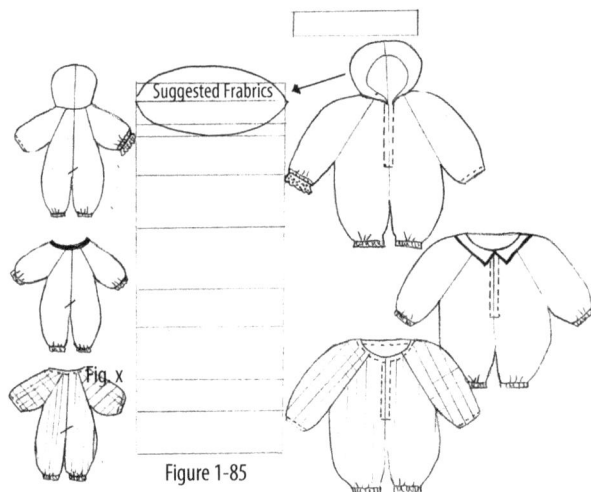

Figure 1-85

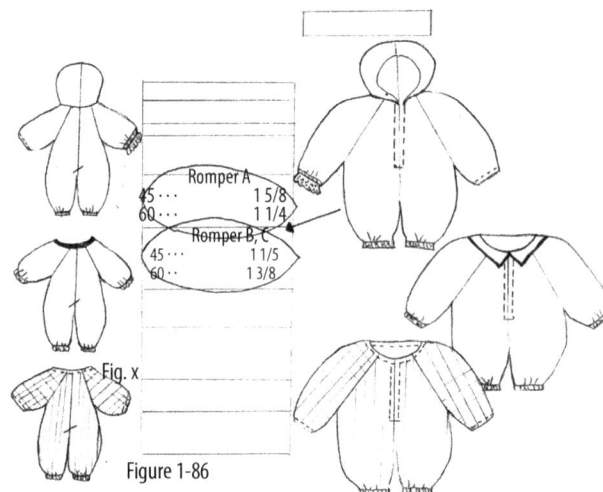

Figure 1-86

Not all fabrics are appropriate for every garment. For example, if your pattern is for a flowing dress, cotton would not be appropriate because it is a stiff fabric. Common fabric types are cotton, cotton blend, polyester, wool, silk, rayon, and challis. There are two types of fabric, natural and man-made.

Natural fibers are cotton, wool, silk, and linen. These fabrics are made from plant or animal products. They "breathe" as air flows through and makes the garments more comfortable to wear year round. A widely used man-made fabric is polyester. It does not breathe. It may look like silk and be lightweight, but it can be hot to wear. Fabrics like polyester that stretch can be harder to sew. Some fabrics can pull and unravel. These are not recommended for early projects.

Some garments call for interfacing. This is a layer of material added to the fabric to stiffen, stabilize, or allow easier handling of the fabric while sewing. Patterns will typically call for interfacing in areas needing extra body for a shirt collar, or strength for buttonholes. When sewing knit fabric, you may choose to use interfacing to keep the fabric from stretching out of shape.

Acetate – This fabric is often used for bridal wear. There are pros and cons to using this fabric. It must be dry cleaned. It stains easily and many stains will not come out. Deodorant will take the color out of the fabric, so if you use this fabric buy underarm protectors (pads). If the wearer will be using perfume, put it on before getting dressed so the perfume is not sprayed directly onto the garment. However, it is a very beautiful fabric. An alternative is to use cotton acetate that looks the same; I recommend this alternative.

Cotton – Fabrics that are 100% cotton will shrink when washed. This is already figured into the amount of fabric your pattern requires. Cotton may wrinkle when you wash it. You can test for this by taking a corner of the fabric, wad it up in your hand, hold it there for a while, and then let it go. If the fabric is wrinkled, it will need to be ironed after washing. Quilts are often made out of cotton.

Denim – There are many types of denim fabrics. Most denims are made out of cotton. Denim comes in various weights: heavyweight, lightweight, very thin, and stretch. Another fabric that looks like light denim is chambray. The difference between denim and chambray lies in the weave itself. Chambray has a much lighter and softer feel than denim, which gives it a unique versatility.

Flannel – This fabric is usually made out of cotton and has a nap (see Nap fabrics later in this list). It shrinks a little more than regular cotton fabric, therefore buy a quarter-of-a-yard more than the pattern recommends. It also has a tendency to unravel.

Fur and Cutting – Nap is the texture of a fabric with the raised fibers of the fabric going in a particular direction. If you are purchasing a nap fabric at a fabric store, be sure to ask for a person who is experienced with how to properly cut nap fabric or much of the nap can be cut away (below).

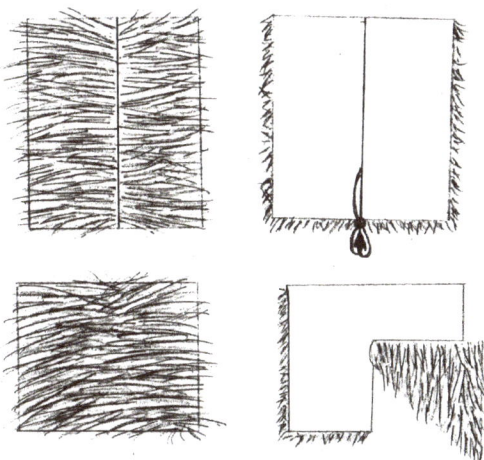

Figure 1-87

Figure 1-88

When you buy nap fabric, the nap is fairly high. When cutting fur, put the fur nap side down on the cutting table and cut from the back (figure 1-88).

Your cutting table can be any table large enough to lay out and cut your fabric. The table should be at a comfortable height that you can stand at. You can buy a cardboard cutting mat so as not to damage your table.

Authors Note:
I used to cut out my fabric pieces on the floor, but my knees don't allow that anymore!

To cut out your pattern pieces, lay the fabric nap side down and pin the pattern pieces **face down** on the backing side (figure 1-89). Draw around the pattern pieces with a pencil, and then cut, pointing the scissors up to separate the fur. Be sure to ONLY cut through backing side of the fabric, NOT all the way through to the fur (see below).

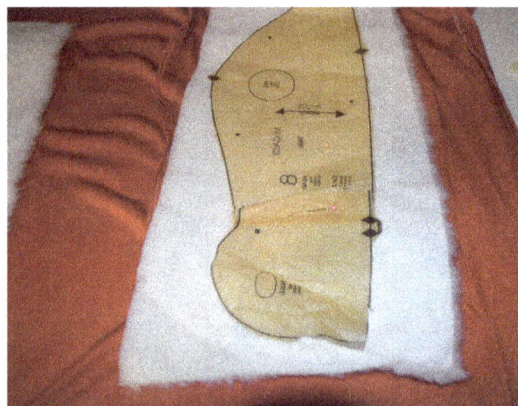

Figure 1-89   Place nap-side down

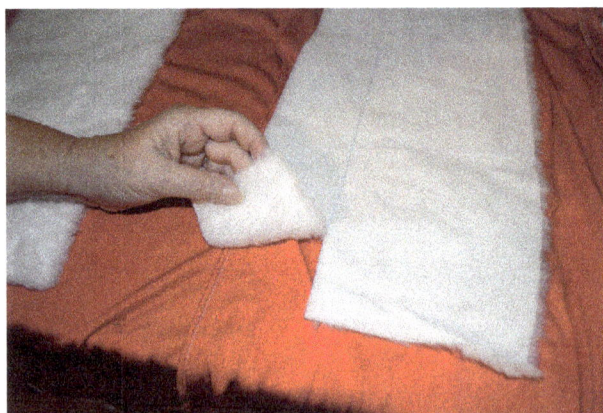

Figure 1-90

Knit or Interlock – A stretch knit can be made from cotton. The pattern may ask for a stretch-knit-only fabric, which is tee-shirt fabric. The bolt will not say "tee-shirt fabric" but will say interlock or knit on the bolt. Jersey is a double-knit fabric.

Swimsuit fabrics and tee-shirt knit fabrics, or anything that has a stretch to it, need to be sewn in a certain way. A type of sewing machine called a serger is excellent for stretch fabrics as it binds the edge of the fabric. However, beginners should not feel the need to buy a serger as this is for advanced sewing. Using your regular sewing machine, you can achieve the same result by sewing two rows of stitching throughout the garment (figure 1-91).

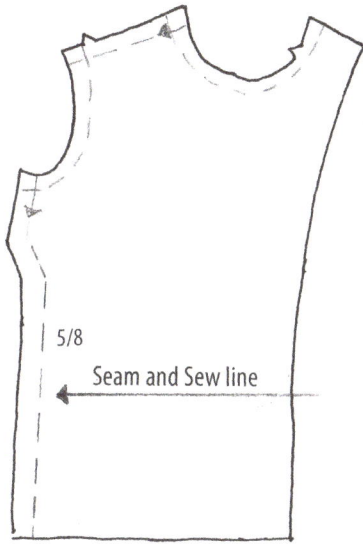

5/8

← Seam and Sew line

Figure 1-91

Most garments with stretch fabrics do not have a zipper. Therefore the garment needs to either pull up from the bottom or stretch over the head. These garments fit close to the body.

Lace – Lace is an easy fabric to work with. The only problem you might have is that it is hard to tell where the selvage is. (Selvages are covered in Section 9.)

Before you lay out the fabric to pin on your pattern pieces, you will need to handbaste fabric layers together (figures 1-92 and 1-93). You can then lay out the pattern pieces and the fabric will not shift.

Linen – This fabric looks like cotton with flex fibers woven through the fabric.

Nap – Corduroy, velvet, and fleece are fabrics that have nap. The best way to understand nap is how you notice, when vacuuming carpet, the look and color seem to change when going in different directions. Nap fabrics do the same; therefore you will need to lay out your pattern pieces all going in the same direction (figures 1-94 and 1-95).

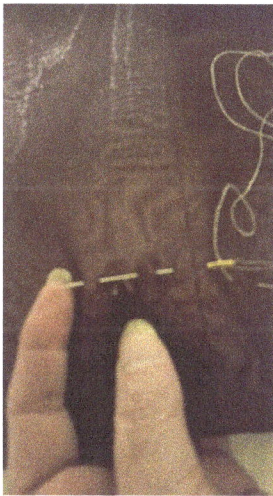

Figure 1-92

Figure 1-93

Figure 1-94

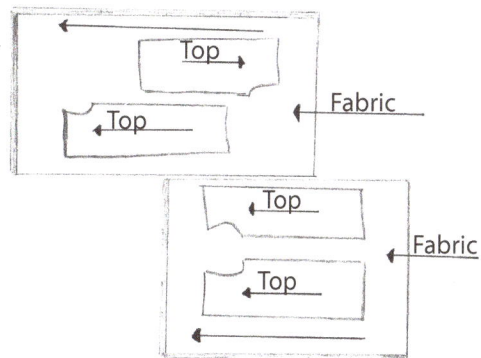

Figure 1-95 One-direction fabric layout

On the back of a pattern envelope you may see little dots, stars, or indentations. The pattern will tell you the meaning of these markings. One dot indicates without nap, two dots indicate with nap, and three dots indicate it doesn't matter. (figure 1-86)

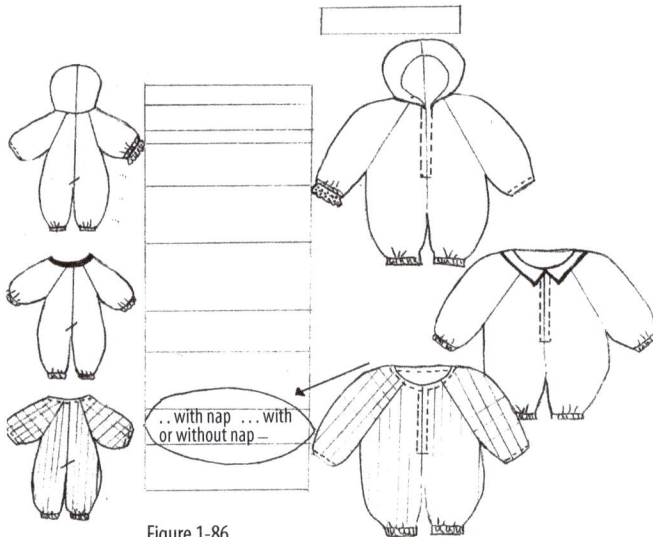

Figure 1-86

Nylon – This is a polyester fabric. A good way to tell if a fabric is nylon is if you have ever had a garment (such as children's pajamas) and the fabric rolls up and can "run," or the wrong needle or pin leaves holes, then it is nylon. This fabric can be a hot fabric to wear as it will not breathe.

Plaids or Repeating Patterns – These fabrics are difficult for beginners. They should be treated like nap fabrics. You will need to buy more fabric than the pattern calls for. Plaids not only have repeating patterns but also have two or more colors. When laying the pattern out to cut, the plaid on one side of each pattern piece must match the plaid on the opposite side or the finished garment will not look correct as the plaid patterns will not match up. Like wallpaper has to match the pattern (below).

Figure 1-97 Plaid must match

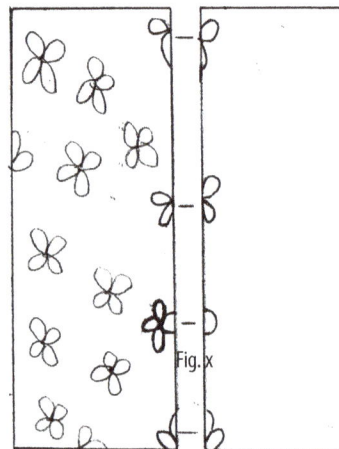

Figure 1-98 Pattern Match similar to wallpaper

Polyester – This fabric is a manmade fiber made from plastic. It will not shrink when washed.

Many fabrics can be a blend, such as cotton and polyester, and those will not shrink.

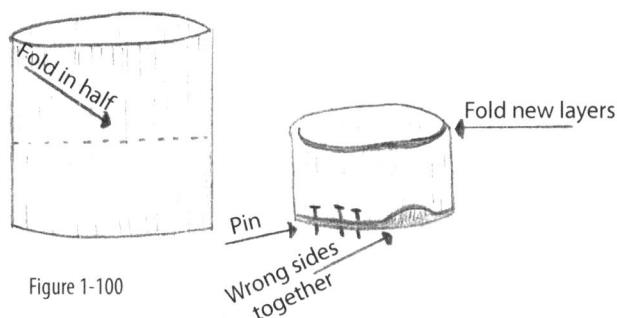

Ribbing – Ribbing is a tube-like fabric with the ridges called ribs. Ribbing is often used on the cuffs, neck, or bottom of sweatshirts and tee-shirts (see left). This makes the garment fit snuggly at those points, while stretching to make the garment easy to put on.

Figure 1-100

This fabric is very easy to sew if you understand how it stretches. Remember, stretch fabric has two rows of stitching in the seams.

Sheer Satin – There are two types of this fabric. One is easy to sew with. You can tell the second type if you put the fabric over your arm and it slides off. This type will be hard to sew and will need to be baste stitched first before cutting it out. This is not a good fabric for a beginner.

Silk – This is a natural fiber and also can be difficult to work with. If you put it on your arm and it slides off, it will also slide when cutting and sewing.

Velveteen and Velvet – The difference between these fabrics is that velveteen is cotton and velvet is acetate. Both are nap fabrics. Velveteen can be ironed by turning it over and ironing on the backside. Use a pillow or something soft underneath the fabric so ironing does not crush the nap and ironing will steam through the fabric. Velvet must be dry-cleaned and you can see the shine on the back of the fabric. There is also stretch Velvet, which is a very heavy fabric and difficult to sew. Long Velvet dresses will need straps as the weight of the fabric will pull a strapless dress down.

Wool – This is a natural fiber and is not hard to work with. It needs to be dry-cleaned only. Many men's suits are made of wool.

Washing Fabric – Be sure to check the end of the fabric bolt (figure 1-101, next page) to verify the width of the fabric (45" or 60"), the type of fabric, and washing instructions. If the fabric

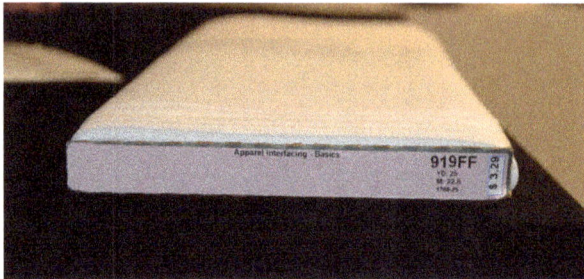

Figure 1-101

is washable, wash it before cutting out your pattern pieces as the fabric may shrink or run after washing. If the dye on the fabric was not completely set, then the colors might run (bleed). If the color runs, return the fabric for a refund.

Interfacing and Lining ———

Interfacing is a stiffening fabric that goes between two layers of fabric to secure an area of a garment. One type of interfacing is available for most fabrics; another for knits which comes in black or white. Interfacing is often used in areas such as necks or collars, waistbands of a skirt or

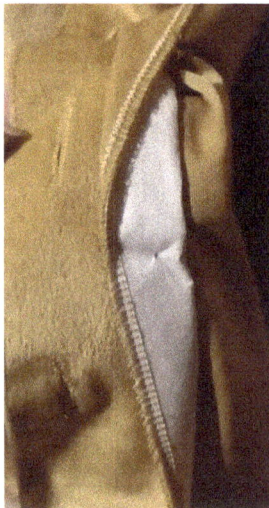

Figure 1-102

pair of pants, and buttonholes on a jacket or shirt (right). For buttonholes, the interfacing keeps the fabric from tearing when buttoning and unbuttoning (left.) Interfacing is also used on hats and anything else that has to be stiffened so that it lays flat and does not wrinkle.

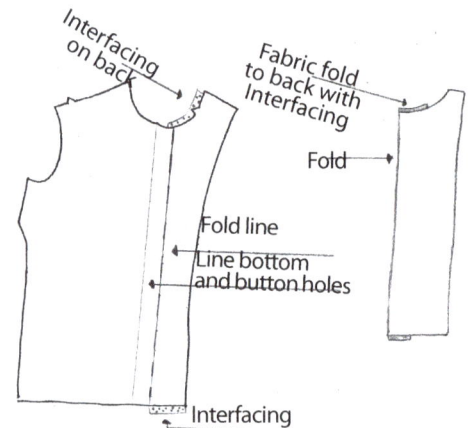

Figure 1-103

Interfacing can be found in fabric stores near the cutting table. Your pattern envelope will tell if interfacing is needed (right). On the end of a fabric bolt (figure 1-101) you will find the weight of that particular interfacing. Heavier fabrics require heavier interfacings. This is also where you can find whether an interfacing is appropriate for knits. Stretch knits require a separate type of interfacing.

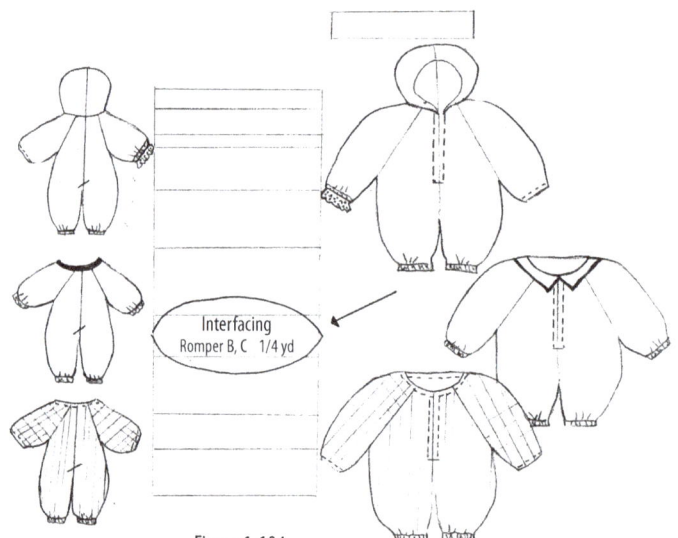

Figure 1-104

There are two categories of interfacing. One has little bumps on it which means you can iron it onto your fabric.

The other kind, without bumps, must be sewn in. You need to pin the interfacing to the garment piece before sewing it into place. The advantage of the sewn versus iron-on interfacing is that if you have to adjust the interfacing, it is easy to do so by just removing the stitches. However, beginners may want to experiment with the iron-on type because it does not slip, which can occur when sewing.

Laying Out Fabric and Pattern Pieces

If using cotton fabric, then use cotton lining because cotton breathes. Do not use polyester fabric with cotton lining.

At the cutting table, you may find flaws in the fabric. If there is not much fabric on the bolt, but the clerk thinks you can cut it to fit, try a different fabric. It is better to buy what the pattern asks for due to shrinkage or mistakes, so best to have enough or maybe a bit more fabric than recommended.

There is a chart near the cutting table which is used for when you want to stay with your chosen fabric that has flaws in it. For example, the fabric is 45″ wide, but only 32″ of it does not have flaws. Have one of the clerks help you use this chart to determine how to still be able to use your chosen fabric (chart below) by adjusting the amount you buy.

Fabric Width	32"	35" - 36"	39"	41"	44"-45"	50"	52"-54"	58"-60"
Yardage	1 7/8	1 3/4	1 1/2	1 1/2	1 3/8	1 1/4	1 1/8	1
	2 1/4	2	1 3/4	1 3/4	1 5/8	1 1/2	1 3/8	1 1/4
	2 1/2	2 1/4	2	2	1 3/4	1 5/8	1 1/2	1 3/8
	2 3/4	2 1/2	2 1/4	2 1/4	2 1/8	1 3/4	1 3/4	1 5/8
	3 1/8	2 7/8	2 1/2	2 1/2	2 1/4	2	1 7/8	1 3/4
	3 3/8	3 1/8	2 3/4	2 3/4	2 1/2	2 1/4	2	1 7/8
	3 3/4	3 3/8	3	2 7/8	2 3/4	2 3/8	2 1/4	2
	4	3 3/4	3 1/4	3 1/8	2 7/8	2 5/8	2 3/8	2 1/4
	4 3/8	4 1/4	3 1/2	3 3/8	3 1/8	2 3/4	2 5/8	2 3/8
	4 5/8	4 1/2	3 3/4	3 5/8	3 3/8	3	2 3/4	2 5/8
	5	4 3/4	4	3 7/8	3 5/8	3 1/4	2 7/8	2 3/4
	5 1/4	5	4 1/4	4 1/8	3 7/8	3 3/8	3 1/8	2 7/8

Figure 1-105 Frabric yardage chart

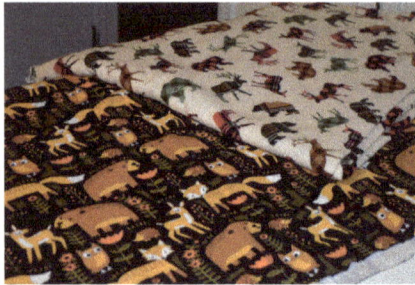

Figure 1-106

Figure 1-107

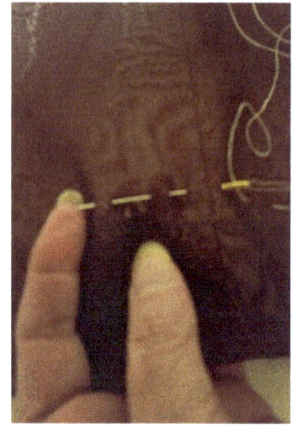

Figure 1-108

If you are working with a fabric that has a plaid or print that goes in one direction, always remember that you will have to match the underneath part and the top part (figures 1-106 and 1-107). You may have to pin your fabric down in sections before laying your tissue pattern on top of it. You may also have to baste stitch all the way through your fabric (figure 1-108) which will save time when sewing a shirt or pair of pants. You want the leg pieces to match (this is where the notches are used) on the right side, left side, back side, and front. If they don't match up, then your finished garment will not match all the way around.

If the fabric is cut incorrectly for the pattern, one leg can be upside down and the other right side up (figure 1-109). When you lay out the fabric, use the notions to help match up your sides (figure 1-110 and 1-111) the same way that wallpaper is laid out.

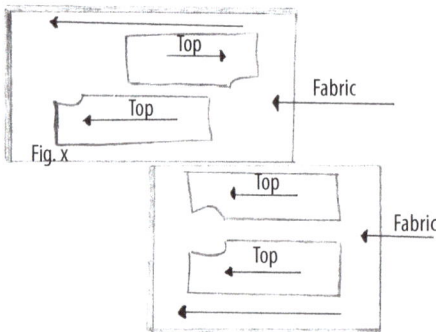

Figure 1-109 One-Direction fabric layout

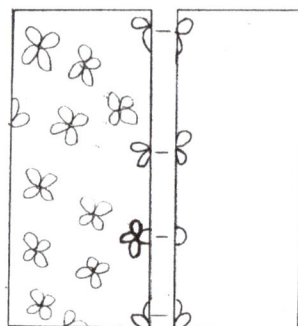

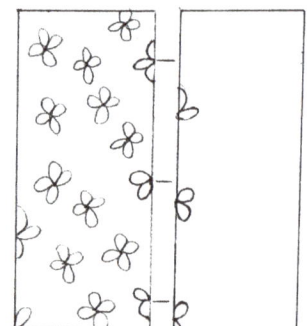

Figure 1-110

The selvage of a piece of fabric is the side that does not stretch. When a piece of fabric is just cut off of the bolt, the selvage is easy to find as it is the top and bottom sides as the fabric is unrolled from the bolt. The selvage is usually a different color than the fabric and might have little holes going through it. (figure 1-111) The key is that this side will not stretch. For fabric just off the bolt this is easy to find.

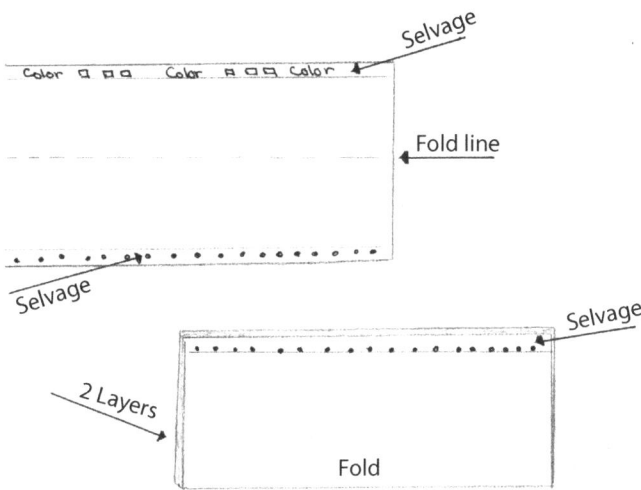

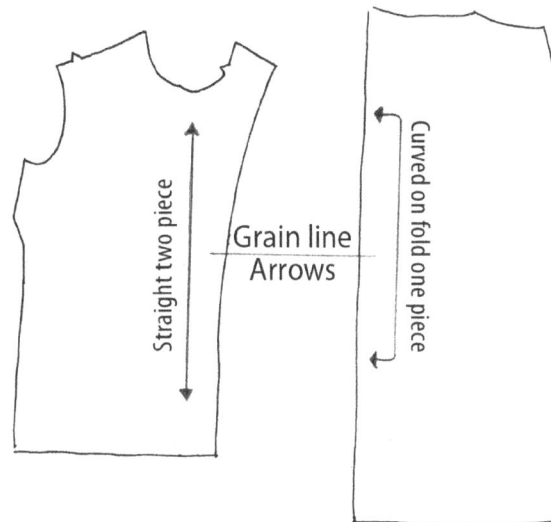

Figure 1-111   Figure 1-112

A grain line on the pattern piece must follow the grain line of your fabric (above).

If you have a piece of fabric that does not include any of the original selvage edges, you can determine the selvage by stretching it along one side, then rotate it a quarter turn and stretch it again. One direction will not stretch; that is the selvage. The other will stretch noticeably.

Open up your pattern envelope and look at the contents. It contains the instructions for layout and the tissue pattern pieces that you will pin onto the fabric to cut out the garment pieces. Look at each pattern piece as well as noting the number of each piece you will need to cut out. Pattern pieces with straight edges are the easiest to cut out and easiest to sew. Curved pieces are a bit more challenging. Review the paper instructions, not the tissue paper pattern pieces, for information about cutting (figure 1-113). This will make it easier to sew (figure 1-114).

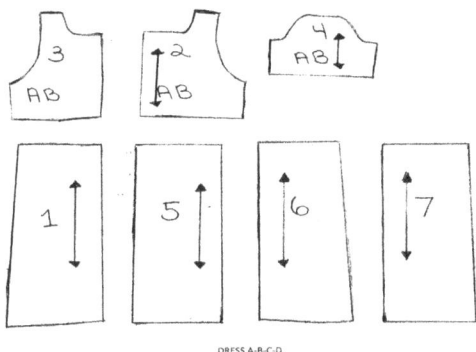

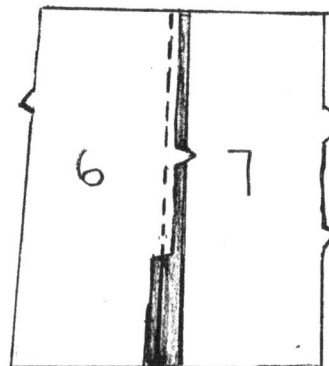

SKIRT SIDE FRONT (6)
TO SKIRT FRONT (7)
Right side together matching notches, then sew seam.

STRAIGHT PATTERN PIECES
ARE EASY TO CUT AND SEW.

Figure 1-113

DRESS A-B-C-D

1. SKIRT BACK
2. BODICE FRONT
3. BODICE BACK
4. SLEEVE A-B
5. SKIRT SIDE BACK
6. SKIRT FRONT
7. SKIRT SIDE FRONT

Figure 1-114

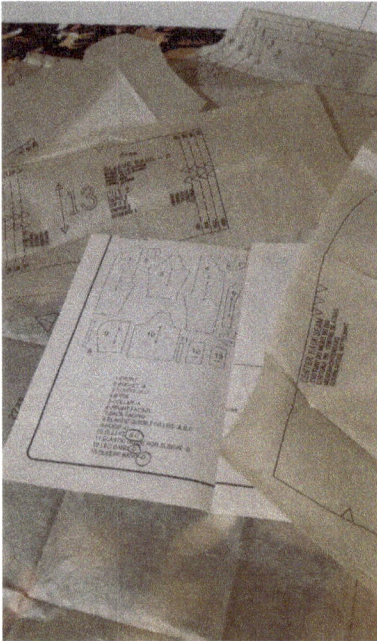

Figure 1-115

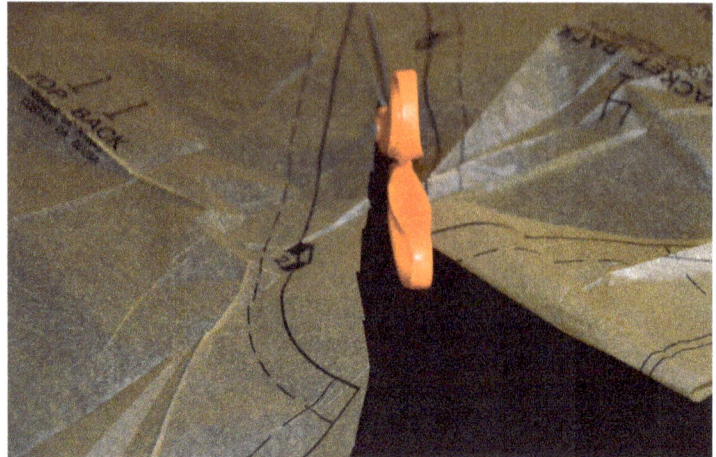

Figure 1-116

Separate the tissue sheets that have the pattern pieces on them (figures 1-115 and 1-116). When initially cutting your tissue pieces apart from the original large tissue sheets from your pattern envelope, DO NOT cut away all the extra tissue from the boundary lines of the pieces. Instead, leave some extra tissue beyond the cutting lines as it is easier to cut out the fabric pieces if you are cutting through tissue and fabric at the same time rather than trying to cut "around" the pattern pieces' cutting lines. In addition, if there is some tissue outside the cutting lines, you can put your non-cutting hand on that to keep tissue and fabric steady as you cut. Fold the pieces not being used and return to the envelope.

Find the view you will be working on as well as the size and width of the fabric required. If it shows 45" width listed three times, that means there are three sizes that can be made from this pattern. The view is identified by letter or the pattern piece example instructions given such as "cut pieces 1 through 4" (figure 1-113, pg 31). The instructions will tell what numbers or letter to look for on the tissue pieces (left).

When looking at the fabric, is the print (front side of the fabric) facing you or is the wrong (back) side facing you? When you fold the fabric, put the right sides of the fabric together with the wrong sides out. If you put the right sides together, it will be faster to sew. You can pin the fabric to sew without having to turn it over (fig 1-118).

Figure 1-117 Letters on each pattern piece

When working with plaid or same directional print, look at the pattern layout section and pictures that are shown. This process takes time. Your instructions will show how to lay out your pattern pieces. Layout is very important to understand. The layout has a color code bar (below). The color bar will show how to lay out the pattern. One is the fabric (black), one is the tissue, and the other can be the interfacing. It shows whether the pattern piece is laid right side up or upside down (figure 1-120).

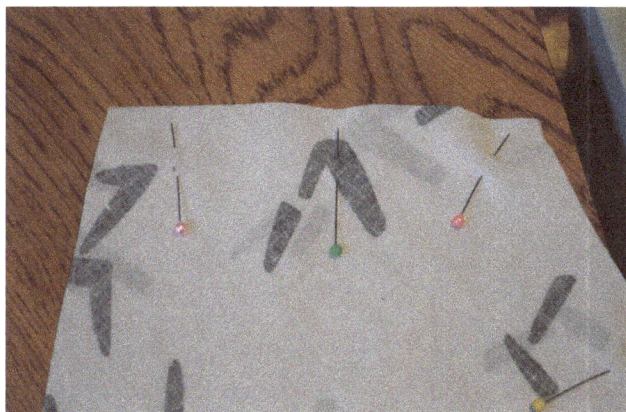

Figure 1-118

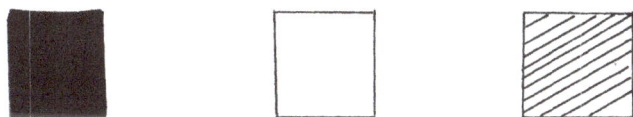

Figure 1-119

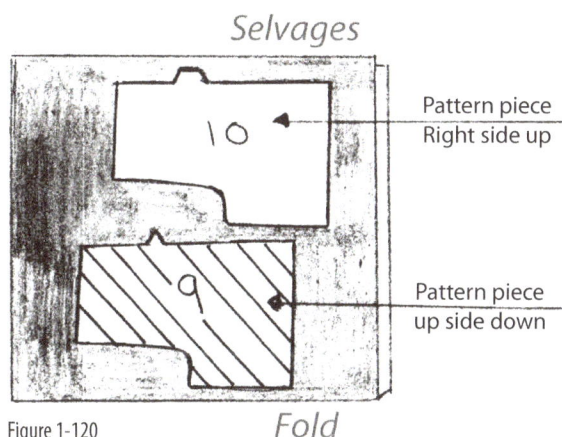

Figure 1-120

The tissue will have everything you need to know about each piece: the number on the front, what view, how many pieces will have to be cut out, and if there is lining. Your tissue will stay pinned on the fabric until you sew it. DO NOT TAKE THE TISSUE OFF the fabric after it is cut out (left).

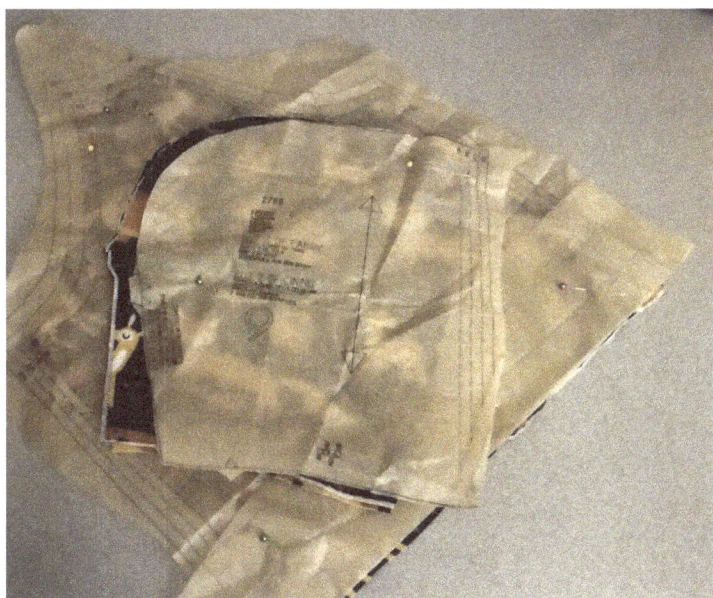

Figure 1-121

Look at the pattern layout section and pictures when working with plaid or same directional print. If there is a big star in your layout, this is important to read. The star shows that the fabric needs to be laid out a different way (below) as the fabric may have a nap. Open your fabric all the way so there is a single layer

Figure 1-122

instead of two when it was folded. Then refold the fabric as shown. If it shows the tissue piece hanging over the fabric (figure 1-123), it is because it is on a fold for cutting out two pieces of fabric. You will have to do these pieces after all the others are already cut.

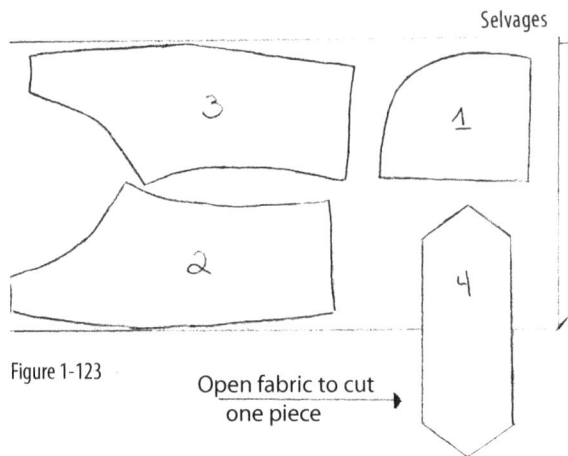
Figure 1-123

Open fabric to cut one piece

If the fabric has a nap, like velvet, the top and bottom need to go the same direction. If the fabric is folded, it has one side going the opposite direction; the top is not going the same direction as the bottom. This will produce problems with the color if the nap is not all going in the same direction. Cut the top piece then turn it 90 degrees so it is going the opposite way see figure 1-124). Put a pin at the top of one piece and when the pinned pieces turn all the way to the other end, they will all be going in the same direction. The right side of your fabric is the brighter print side.

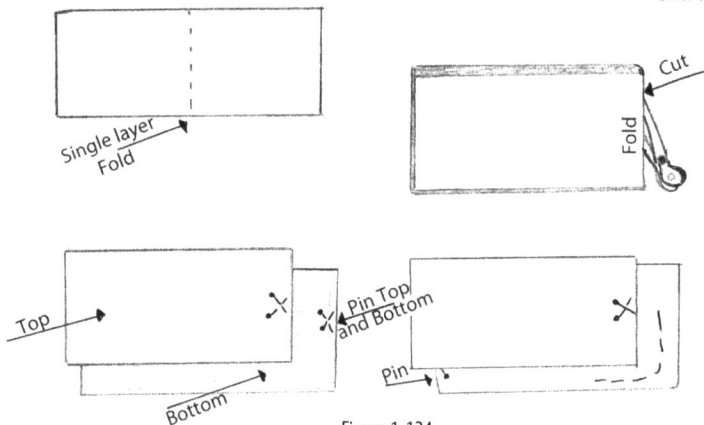
Figure 1-124

Alterations, to a pattern if you are either longer or shorter, (torso or legs) need to be made on the tissue before cutting out fabric to shorten fold the tissue and pin the tissue to the size. Pin the tissue down to the line

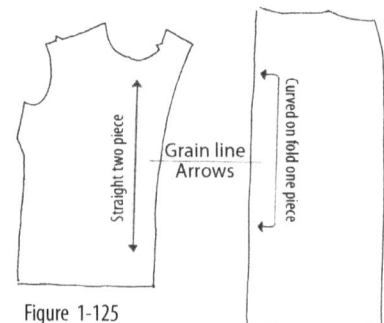
Figure 1-125

going across the tissue; this is the selvage line (right). Following the pattern directions can be confusing for alterations to lengthen, do not cut the tissue first, place it on the fabric then pin the top area so it will not move.

Now cut tissue and move it down to adjust size and pin in place (figure 1-126). If by looking at a pattern you want to adjust it, never adjust at the waist. When you see a person's pants legs really wide at the bottom, it is because they have been shortened from the bottom; the leg should be tapered. This alteration line will make it longer or shorter by folding it or cutting the line (figure 1-127). You can adjust at the hip or at the hem. For pants, you can make them longer or shorter (figures 1-127, 1-128, and 1-130). As shown on the envelope that the alterations have been done for you and has a short or long sleeve.

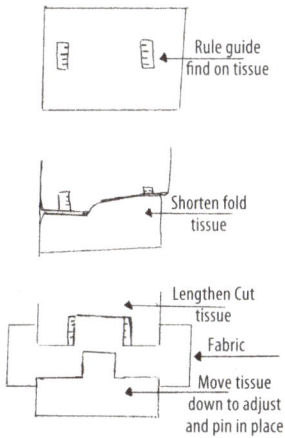
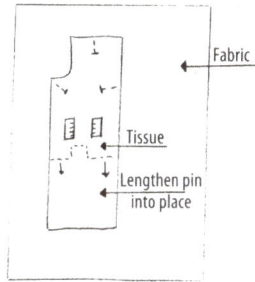
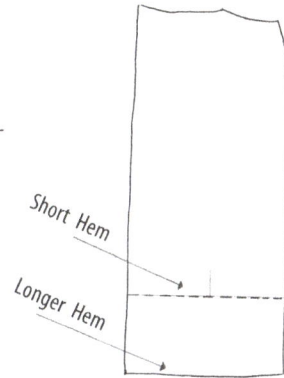

Figure 1-126   Figure 1-127   Figure 1-128

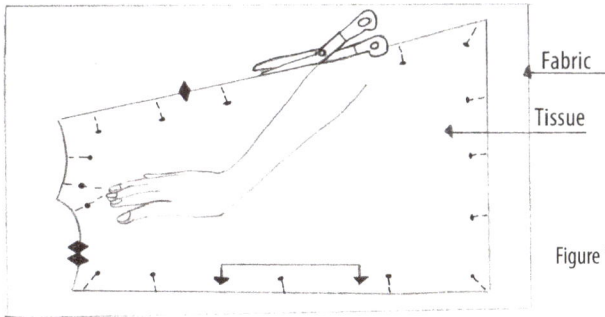

Figure 1-129

Figure 1-130

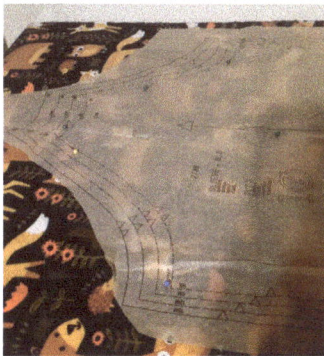

Figure 1-131

Pin down the tissue to anchor it to the fabric, placing the pin inside the line (figure 1-128 and 1-130). Place the pins about every 3 inches so the tissue is not loose while cutting the fabric. The cutting line is the solid line going all the way around the pattern piece. The broken line is a sew line. You will see different lines for different sizes (NB) dash-dot, (6M) dash-dish,

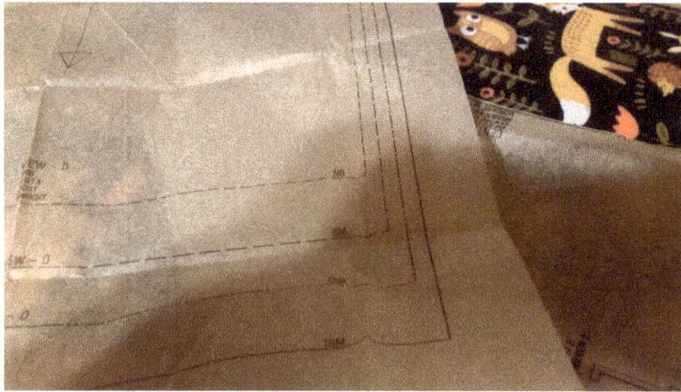

Figure 1-132

(12M) dash long-small dash- small dash and (18M) solid line. Find your size and use that line to cut out your pieces (figure 1-132).

Pattern pieces may have three or four sets of lines, each for a different size, using a broken line, solid line, or dotted line. Use a highlighter to mark the lines for your size on the tissue pieces before beginning to pin to the fabric.

Pinning

Fold the fabric into two layers with the two selvage edges together and a fold at the opposite side of the folded fabric. You may have to fold the layout selvage edges different ways (figure 1-133). Then pin the pattern tissue pieces to the fabric, pinning tissue pieces that say "cut one" on the

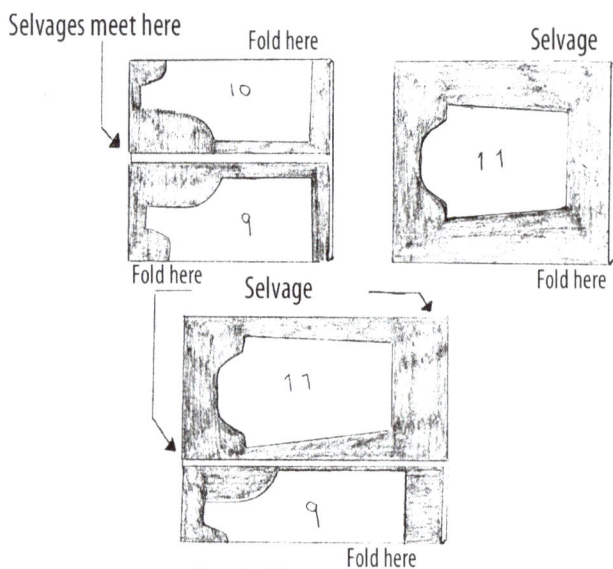

Figure 1-133

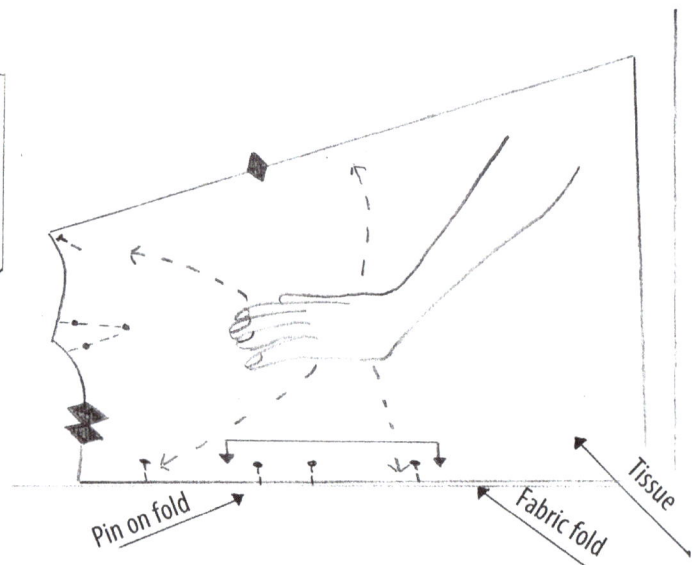

Figure 1-134

fold so that when cut and opened up there will be one piece with the part on each side of the fold matching the other (figure 1-134). DO NOT CUT the fold.

For tissue pieces that say "cut two," lay those on the grain line (figure 1-135).

It is easiest to lay out all your pattern pieces on the fabric and put just a few pins in each pattern tissue piece until you have determined that all pieces are correctly laid out. If not, then adjustments can be time consuming if you have to take all the pins out (figure 1-129, pg 35).

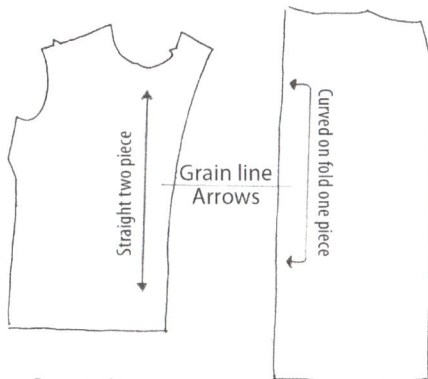

Once you have verified that your layout is correct, by pinning one pin, it will make it easier to move and adjust. (figure 1-136) Use a tape measure to measure from the fold of the fabric to the end of the grain line on the tissue (like a level) at both ends of the grain line (figure 1-138). After all measurements are correct, then pin the pattern pieces down so they cannot shift. The best way to pin is to work from the center, moving your hand out to the

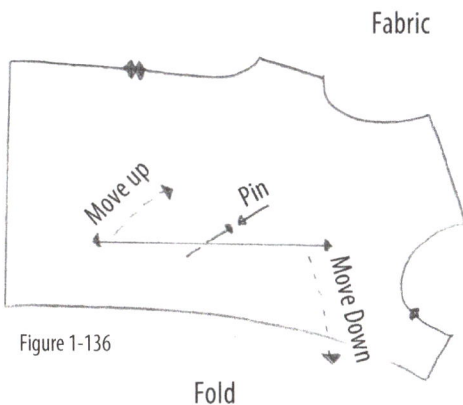

Figure 1-135

Figure 1-136

Figure 1-137 To pin, work from the center

Figure 1-138 Measure from grain line

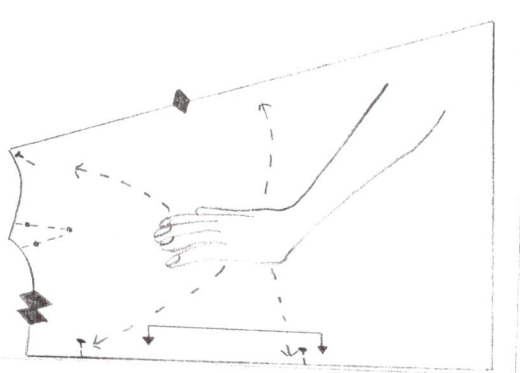

sides as you pin (figure 1-137). The best way to pin through the layers of fabric is at an angle. Put your hand on the fabric to hold it in place. It will be easier to lift up slightly to go through both layers. Pin all corners and fold line so there is no slack (figure 1-129 pg 35).

Pin each pattern piece to the fabric on the inside of

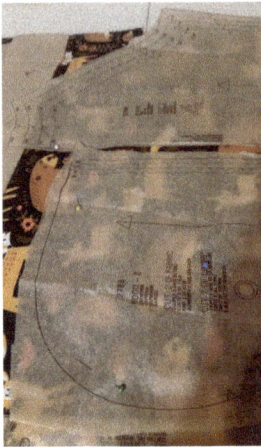

the cutting line (right), do not pin on the outside of the cutting line. Take your time cutting out the fabric pieces as errors can result in not having enough fabric to complete your garment. As you cut out the pieces of fabric, the extra tissue can be discarded.

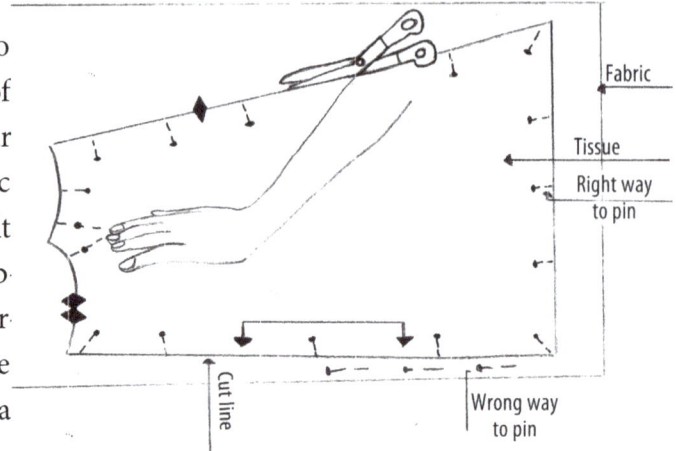

Figure 1-139

Figure 1-140

For cutting, if you do not have a serger (a sewing machine that finishes off the edge of the fabric) you will need to use pinking shears (figure 1-141). Then your fabric will not unravel when it is washed. If it is Polyester, it will not unravel. Can cut out with regular Dressmaker's shears.

Cutting Out Fabric Pieces _____

For cutting fabric, you need to know how to best use your scissors. Many assume that taking big, long cuts is correct. On the contrary, short cuts are best for cutting fabric. As you cut

Figure 1-141

along the cutting lines, take short cuts and do not completely close the scissors after each cut. Cut as close to the cutting line as possible. Keep the fabric flat on the cutting surface by placing one hand on the pattern piece when cutting, and moving that hand as you cut around each piece to stabilize each area as you cut.

Notches – A notch is a small, half-diamond shape (figures 1-142, 143, 144, and 145). Some patterns will show notches with a full diamond. Your measurement size will tell which diamond you will cut out.

Cut notches outward so you can see them when sewing them together. If notches are cut inward, that will cut fabric away from the seam allowance and cause tearing (figures 1-146 and 1-147). If there are two or more diamonds in a row do not cut each one out individually. Instead, cut

Figure 1-142

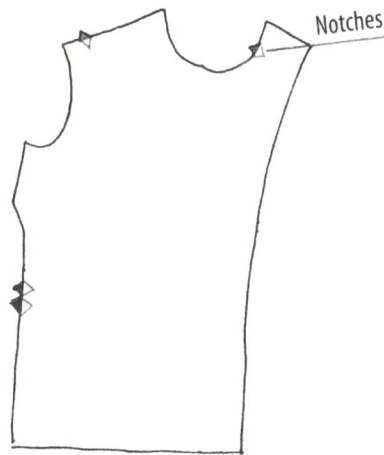

Notches

Figure 1-143

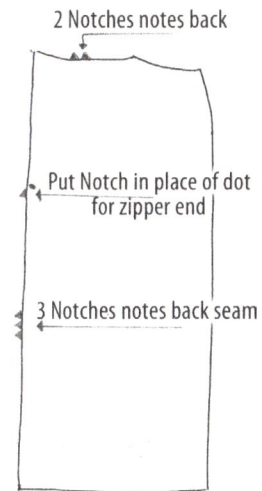

2 Notches notes back

Put Notch in place of dot for zipper end

3 Notches notes back seam

Figure 1-144

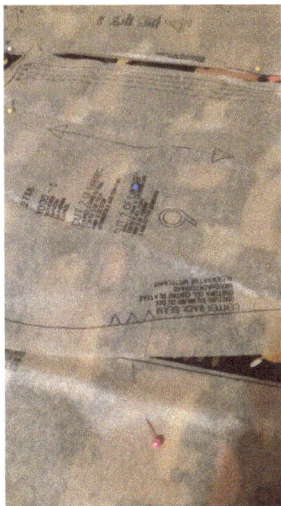

Figure 1-145

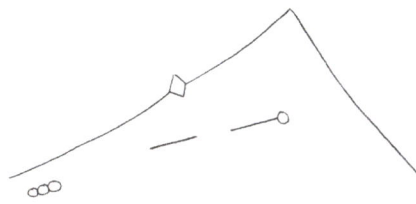

Figure 1-146

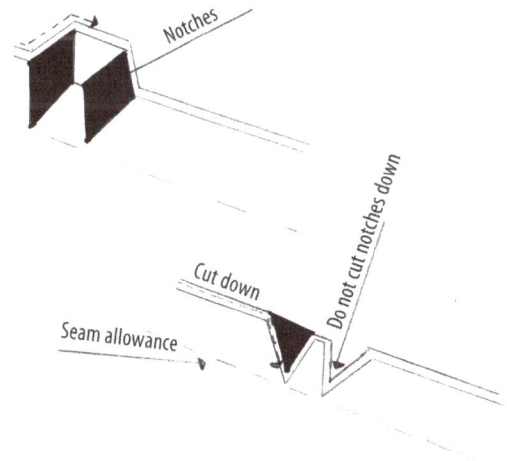

Notches

Cut down

Seam allowance

Do not cut notches down

Figure 1-147

up the first diamond, across the tops of all the diamonds, then down the last diamond. Cut the multiple diamonds as a single unit (figure 1-147).

When cutting out a sleeve cap, which is the top where the shoulder seam is, there is a larger circle on the tissue pattern piece to cut a notch above the circle. This makes it easier to set in the sleeve and will help you see the diamond or notch when the tissue is taken off the fabric.

This notch indicates what you will be matching the fabric to on the other pattern piece which has the same number of notches. Keep the tissue on the fabric until your sew it. You will then be able to tell the back, front, and sides of the sleeve.

Notches are very important in sewing because without them you would not be able to match up the pieces of each part of the garment.

Cutting Jagged Edges – When you are cutting fabric and come to a part of the pattern that has a jagged area or points (figure 1-148), be sure not to cut past the low point. At that point, turn your scissors to cut up. If you keep cutting down, you will cut into the seam allowance. One way to get sharp points at the bottom is to cut to the low point from one side, then reverse your scissors to cut from the next high point back to the previous low point.

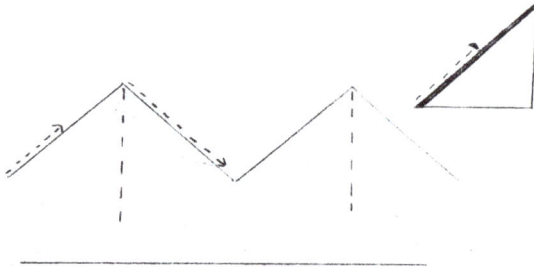

Figure 1-148

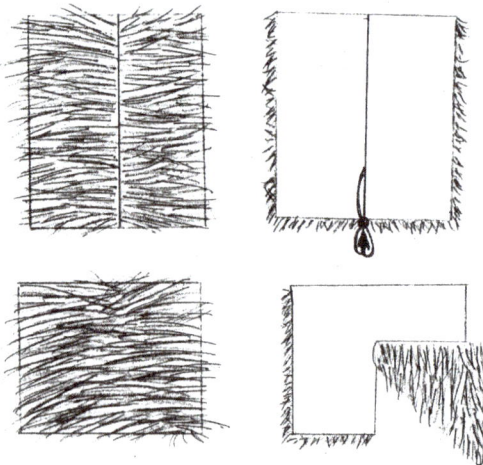

Figure 1-149 Sewing seams on fur

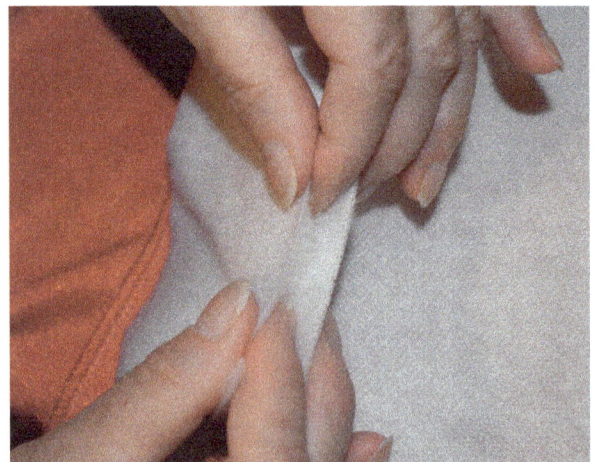

Figure 1-150

When sewing a seam on fur fabric (above), after sewing, use a pin to fluff up the fur fibers to hide the seam line (figure 1-151, next page).

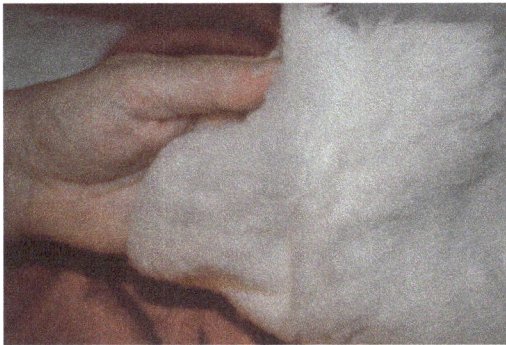

Figure 1-151 Fluff the fibers to hide the seam line

Tailor Tacking ———

There are several ways to tailor tack to mark your fabric before beginning to sew. Tailor tacking will show where to pin and sew to match up your garment pieces. After marking your fabric, it will have markings on the outer part of the pieces with notches (below). Use tailor tacking anywhere it will help you complete your

project successfully, such as the locations for buttons and buttonholes, pockets, etc. Always leave the tissue pattern pieces on the fabric until you begin to sew. Otherwise you may confuse the back with the front or other locations for a garment piece.

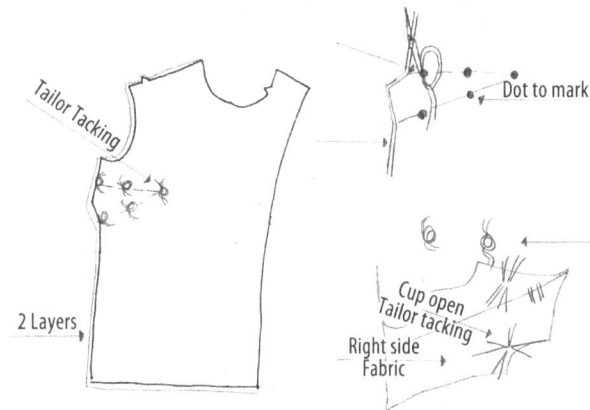

Figure 1-152 Tailor tack where needed

Remember that the pattern tells you every thing you need to know about the fabric piece when you start to sew: where interfacing is needed, where the notches are, where the pockets are to be located, etc. Pattern tissue can be reused, so once you have finished your garment, fold up the pattern pieces and return them to the envelope in case you want to make that same garment at another time.

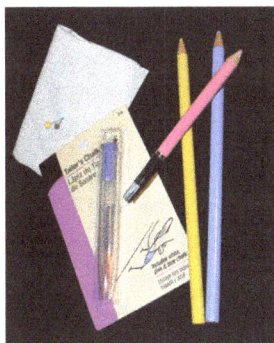

Figure 1-153 Marking pencils

One way to make tailor tack markings on your fabric is to use chalk which looks like a pencil and comes in different colors (left). Along with using chalk, you may also want

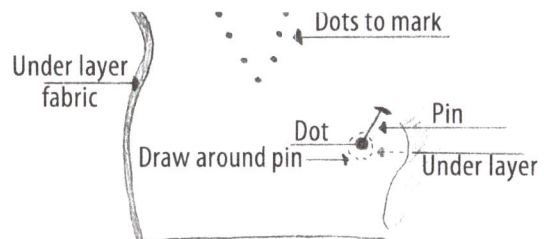

Figure 1-154 Marking the fabric

to use pins which are used to pin through all layers of fabric and then mark around the pins (above). Note that sometimes chalk does not wash out, so if using chalk on a light-colored fabric, choose a light-colored chalk that you can see but hopefully will not leave a dark mark after washing. You also want to be careful with your markings to make sure they are only where needed so unnecessary markings won't remain after your garment is completed.

Figure 1-155 Marking fabric with wheel and tracing paper

Another way to mark your fabric is with a tracing wheel and colored tracing paper (left). The tracing wheel looks like a small pizza cutter with little teeth on it. You put a colored piece of tracing paper between your fabric and the pattern tissue, then roll the wheel across the lines and the wheel marks little dots on your fabric. If you put the tracing paper between two facing sides of fabric it will mark both of them.

A third option is to use thread to mark your fabric. While this method takes a bit longer, it has several advantages. When using thread, you do not have to worry about chalk or tracing paper marks not washing out. You can

Figure 1-156 Marking fabric with thread

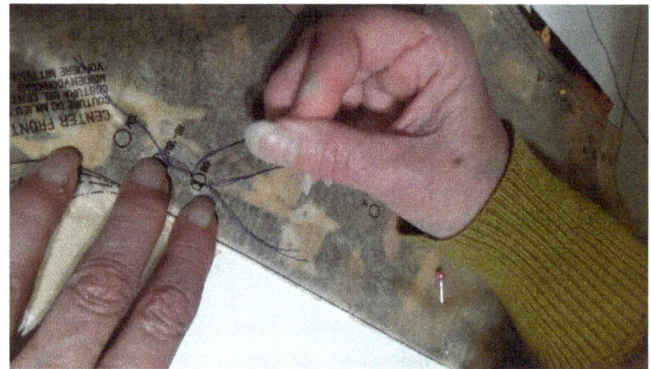

Figure 1-157

use different colored thread so you can choose a color that will show up clearly against your fabric, and by using thread you can mark several layers of fabric at one time. (figure 1-157)

When marking with thread, thread your needle leaving two loose ends (right). Do not tie a knot at the end of the two loose ends as you will eventually pull out all threads when they are no longer needed. Find the dots on the tissue pattern piece. Start on the side of the circle with your needle and thread. Bring your needle through to the other side of the circle. Leave a long tail of thread (figures

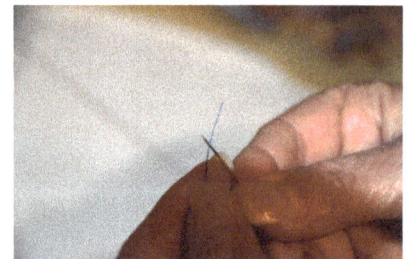

Figure 1-158

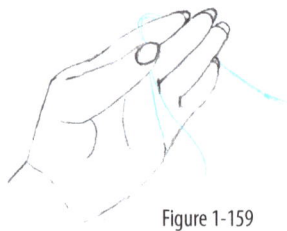

Figure 1-159

1-160 through 1-163). Now go back through the same hole and out the same hole, forming a loop (figures 1-164 and 1-165). Repeat this process at all you're inside marks on the circle because eventually you are going to take off the tissue paper in order to sew. After you have tacked the tissue, drag the needle or a pin through the little hole where you made the loop of your tailor tack. This separates the tissue so the loop can come completely through the paper

Figure 1-160

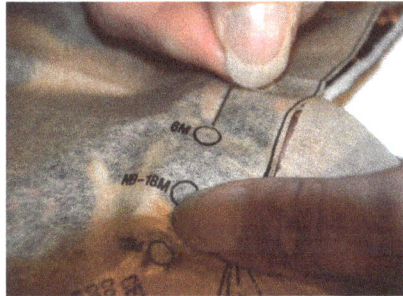

Figure 1-161

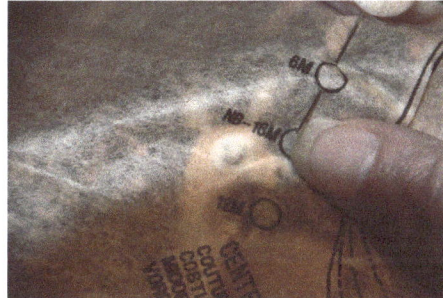

Figure 1-162

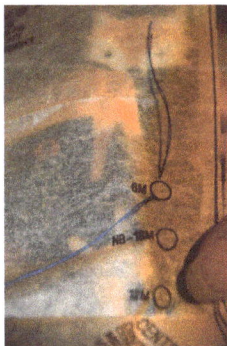

Figure 1-163

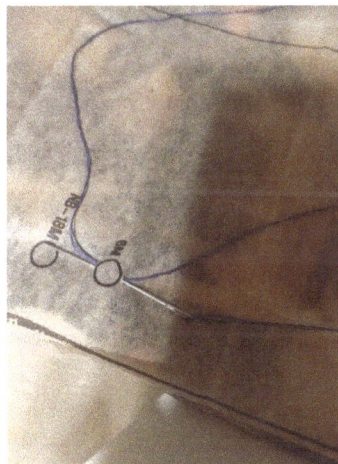

Figure 1-164

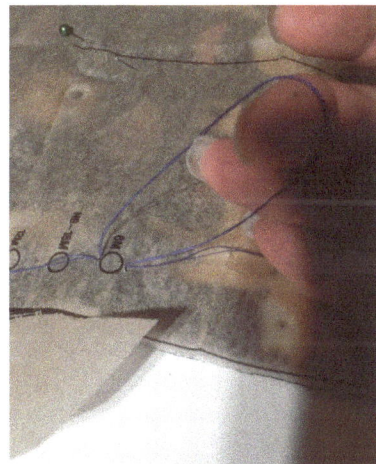

Figures 1-165

Figure 1-166

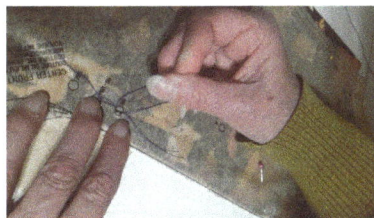

Figure 1-167

Figure 1-168

(figures 1-166, 167, and 168). The tissue will pull right off your fabric, leaving the tailor tack on the fabric. Cut the thread between each layer of fabric (top, next page). Now you have markings on all sides of your fabric.

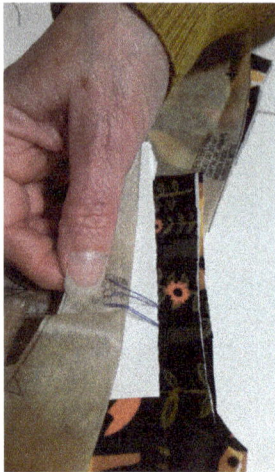

Figure 1-169

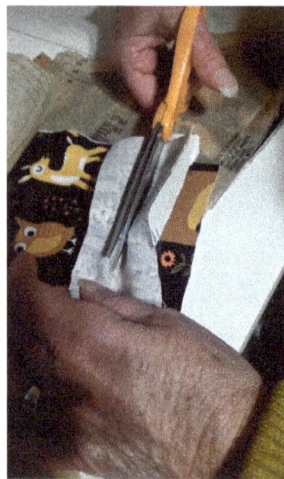

Figure 1-170

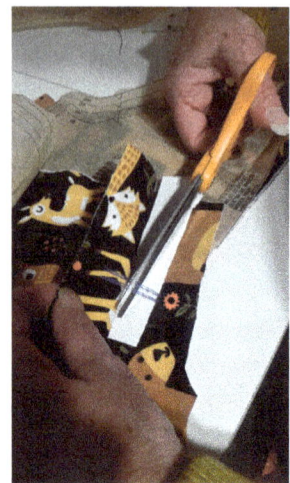

Figure 1-171

After you have checked all the above pictures of the three types of marking for tailor tacking, you may want to try each on a sample piece of fabric to determine which works best for you.

Problems with Sewing Machines

Most problems with your sewing machine occur when fabric suddenly jams underneath the presser foot. If your machine jams, stop sewing and raise up the presser foot which will release the tension on the thread. You may need to rethread your machine. Use scissors to cut away fabric or threads in the jam area, taking care to only cut the fabric if it will not make a hole in the garment. Take out the bobbin and clean out the area (figure 1-172) where the bobbin was inserted. Do not take all the parts out around the bobbin, which is the casing that holds the bobbin in place (figure 1-173). Clean up the area where you were sewing as there may be loose threads stuck in the area of the jam. Make sure there is no incorrect threading as shown in the following pictures (figures 1-174 and 1-175). Then rethread the machine and begin sewing where you left off.

Figure 1-172

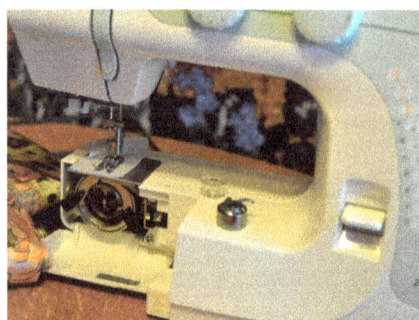

Figure 1-173

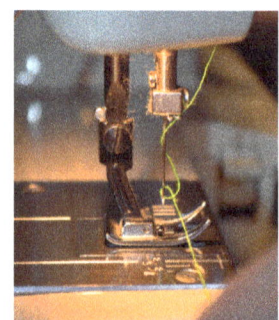

Figure 1-174

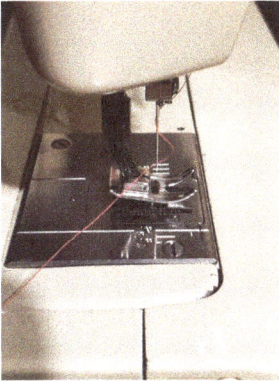

Figure 1-175

Figure 1-176

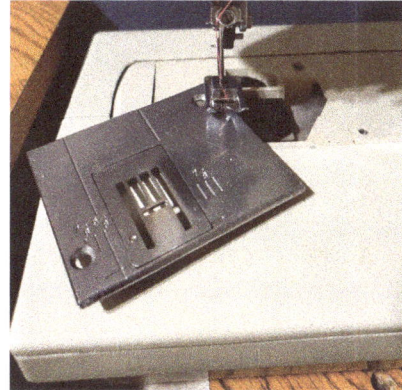

Figure 1-177

Another problem area can be if you notice lint collecting around the presser foot. The best way to clean out lint is with a can of air. You can also use a can of air to clean out the area where the feed dogs show through the throat plate (figure 1-176) as lint there can also cause a jam. The throat plate can be removed to clean out that area as well (figure 1-177). A good practice is to use the can of air to clean out all these areas on a regular basis to avoid future jams.

Check your thread take-up lever (figure 1-178) to make sure the thread is still on correctly as that can also cause a jam. If so, first lift the presser foot, and then turn the hand wheel (figure 1-179) toward you, and gently pull the fabric, which should release the fabric from the machine. Cut any loose threads, and then begin to sew.

Check your manual for parts of your machine where you may need to add machine oil. Not all machines require this. If your machine recommends using oil, it is suggested that it be added after every 8 hours of use. Be sure, after adding oil, that you use a scrap piece of fabric to sew on so that any extra oil is absorbed before you return to sewing on your garment fabric. Otherwise, the oil will stain your fabric.

Figure 1-178 Thread take-up lever

Figure 1-179 Hand wheel

Your sewing machine has a light in it. Always use this when sewing so you can clearly see your stitches as they are being made. Sewing machine lights have different types of bulbs. Some may screw in; others may just pop in. When your bulb has burned out, remove it and take it to a fabric store so that you purchase the correct bulb for your machine.

SEWING FOR SUCCESS

AN ILLUSTRATED GUIDE FOR BEGINNERS

PART TWO

Let's Start Sewing!

Start to Sew ———

When starting to sew a garment, make sure not to attempt projects beyond the skills of a beginner. Most beginners want to start to make something that can be difficult, such as a garment that has a collar, buttons, pockets, and sleeves.

Start small, with a simple pattern, while you get comfortable with your machine. A basic skirt can be a good beginner project. It has a zipper, interfacing, seams, and a hem. Shorts or pants with an elastic waistband can also be appropriate for a beginner, as can be a pull-over top, or something that has a simple sleeve.

A pattern envelope shows how many pieces you will need to sew together and how difficult it will be. For example, a garment that has a lot of curves and many different pieces may be too difficult for a beginner. To start , the simpler the pattern and the fewer the pieces, the easier it is to complete the garment and gain confidence in your beginning sewing skills (2-1 and 2-2).

When I teach in a classroom, I like to present simple things like showing how to sew on a button. It does not have to be for a garment itself; it can be practice on fabric scraps. Getting some inexpensive zippers and practicing sewing them on scrap fabric is a great way to learn that skill before you try to sew in a zipper on a garment you plan to wear. It is best to try out different sewing challenges on scrap fabric first.

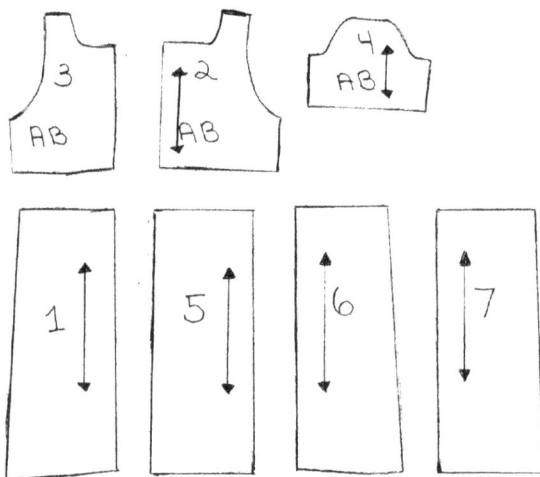

Figure 2-1

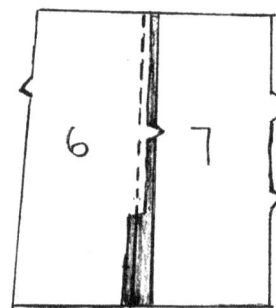

Figure 2-2

Match Up Your Notches. If your notches do not match up when sewing, your garment will not be properly aligned when finished. Find the notches on the back and front pieces of your pattern (figure 2-3).

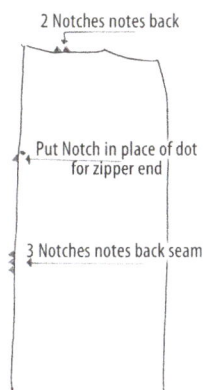

2 Notches notes back

Put Notch in place of dot
for zipper end

3 Notches notes back seam

Figure 2-3

Figure 2-4

Figure 2-5

It makes no difference which direction you are sewing as long as when you are sewing, the main part of your fabric is on the outer part of your sewing machine (figures 2-4 and 2-5) and not bunched up inside the machine area.

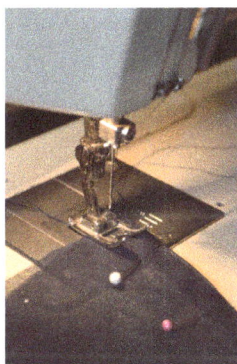

Figure 2-6

Note that most sewing machines are made for right-handed persons. Therefore, if you are left-handed it may take a bit of time to get comfortable having to use your right hand for many of the adjustments that you have to make – such as using the hand wheel, threading your machine and bobbin, adjusting stitch length, etc. Your fabric will mostly hang off the left-hand side of your machine and not on the right side. Start at the top with the fabric on the outer left-hand side (figure 2-6) and remember to guide your fabric with your left hand as you sew; do not pull the fabric (figure 2-5).

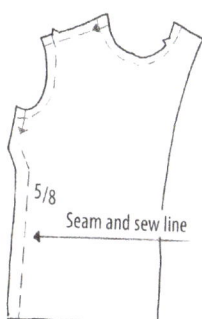

5/8

Seam and sew line

Figure 2-7

Stretch Fabrics. When sewing on swimsuit fabric, tee-shirt knit, and any fabric that has a stretch to it, these fabrics require a specific sewing technique. If you do not have a sewing machine that is a serger, which binds the edges of your fabric, you will need to make two rows of stitching at all seams (figure 2-7). First use the normal 5/8" seam stitch, and then sew another set of stitches very close to it on the inside of that seam. The inside is closer to the cut edge than your first seam

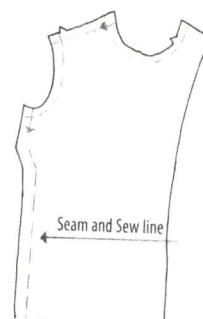

Seam and Sew line

Figure 2-8

stitches (figure 2-8). Be sure when you sew the first set of seam stitches that you are following the guide line for 5/8" on the throat plate (figure 1-76 pg 45). The reason for the double stitching is that the second row takes stress off the first row of stitches when the fabric is stretched.

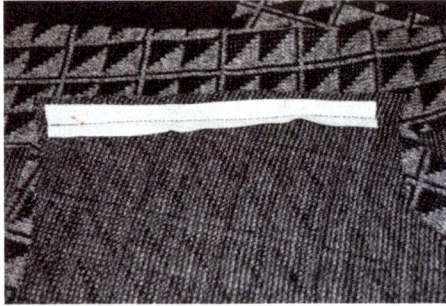
Figure 2-9

Otherwise, with only one row of stitching, when stitches break it will leave small holes in the seam.

Another option when sewing on stretch fabric is to use bias tape and line it up where you are going to sew a shoulder area (left). This will keep that area from losing its shape over time when stretched as it will not stretch out or pucker.

Figure 2-10

Seams need to be pressed open, however it may not be convenient each time to get out an iron and ironing board. An alternative that works particularly well with cotton fabric is to finger press the seam (left). Using one of your finger nails, rub down on the seam to make it lay flat which is what using an iron does. When using an iron, you need to be sure that your iron is not too hot for the fabric. If so, the iron can leave burn marks on the fabric. If ironing, place a piece of cotton cloth over the open seam, then iron. The cotton cloth can be dry or damp. This protects the fabric during ironing. This technique is particularly useful when working with delicate fabrics, such as silk or anything with polyester in it as polyester can melt from the heat of an iron. Using steam from an iron will give a crisp hem or pleat in pants, skirts, dresses, etc. You want to do that before hemming so that the hem will be even. Slightly wet the cotton cloth, then lay it over the garment and steam the hem or pleat.

Darts

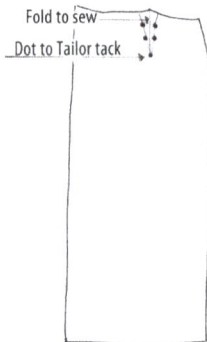
Figure 2-11

Darts can be found in bust lines, skirts, dresses, and pants to contour the fabric to a person's shape (left). For example when making a skirt, the waistband is smaller than the hips, therefore the skirt will need darts or elastic (right) or it will not fit smoothly over the hips.

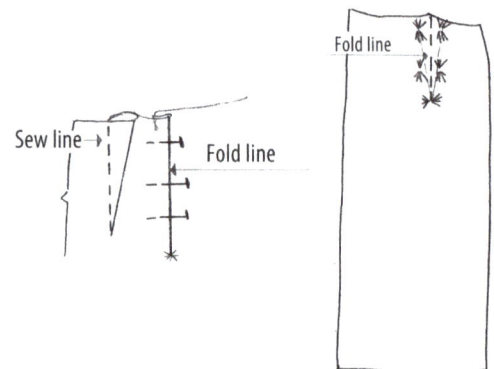
Figure 2-12

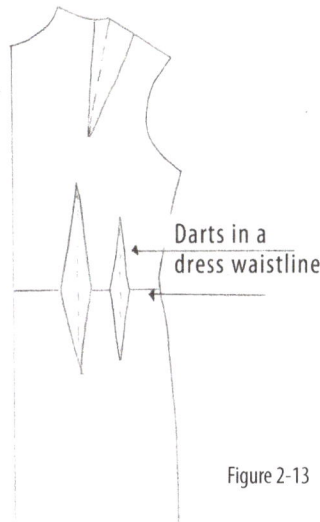

Darts in a dress waistline

Figure 2-13

Dresses have darts in the back, and they may also have them through the waist area (left). Darts are very important to use if making a garment for a busty person. Darts can take care of gaps under the arm. When a sleeveless outfit gaps when sewn, it means darts are needed in that area. Darts are easy to sew (figure 2-12).

Tailor tacking can be used to mark where darts belong on the fabric (right). Because a dart needs to come to a sharp point, do not end the seam with the reverse button to lock the threads in place. Instead, when you get to the end of the dart, continue to sew off the fabric. Then allow for longer threads before cutting the thread from the machine. You will tie a knot at the end of the threads instead of backstitching so the dart does not come undone when the garment is worn (figures 2-15 and 2-16).

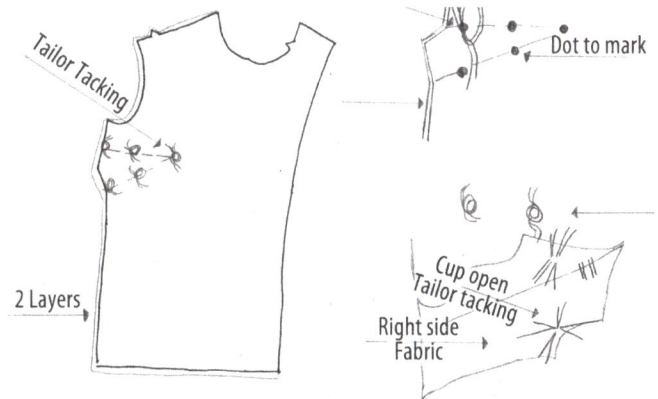

Figure 2-14

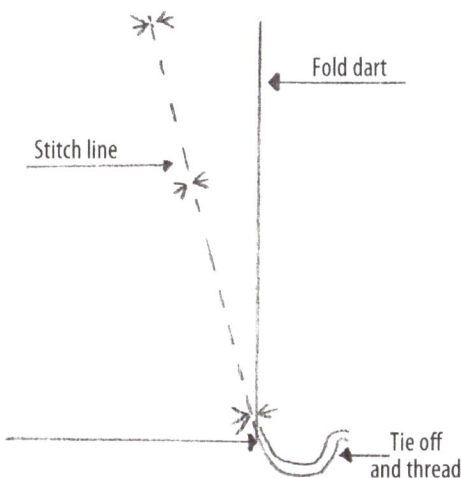

Figure 2-15

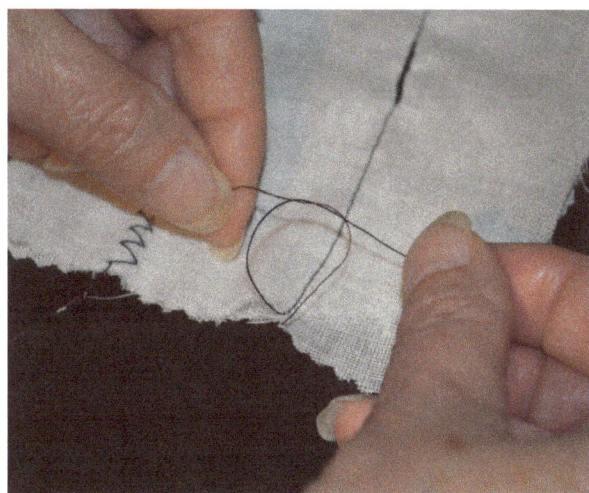

Figure 2-16

Elastic _____

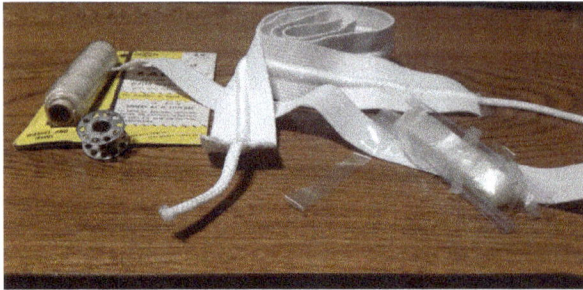

Figure 2-17 Different types of elastic

There are several types of elastic made for different fabrics. Soft elastic is used for undergarments and slips. If a garment needs to be dry-cleaned, it will need elastic that will not rot or dry out. Cotton elastic can be bleached or dry-cleaned and is off-white in color.

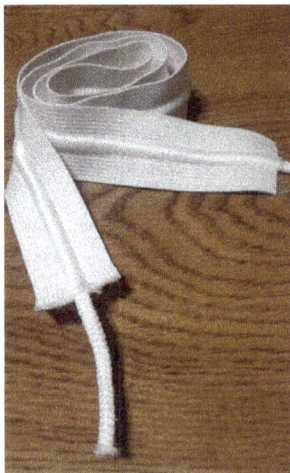

Figure 2-18 Elastic with drawstring

Polyester elastic works for almost any garment except that you cannot bleach it. If bleached, it will not last long as it will crack and dry out.

There is elastic which has a drawstring sewn in it (left) that is used in pants or pajamas. There is also a clear elastic (right), which is my favorite to use, especially for small items like doll clothes. Made for swimwear, it is elastic that can be stretched and will then return to its original shape without

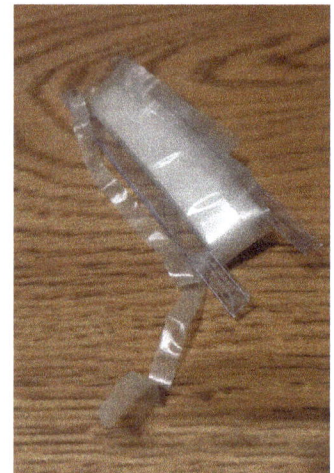

Figure 2-19 Clear elastic

popping stitches. Most elastic will use a zigzag stitch (left) which looks like an accordion. This versatile elastic has many different uses, such as keeping garments from slipping off hangers and on the straps of bras. When pulling on this elastic, the threads also pull but will not break.

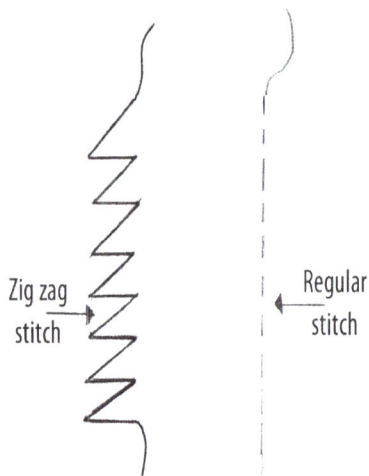

Zig zag stitch

Regular stitch

Figure 2-20 Two types of stitches

There is one other elastic which can be used in a bobbin (figure 2-21). This is the only elastic that can be wound onto the thread bobbin, but must be wound using only the hand wheel without tension. Use this elastic as you would use thread.

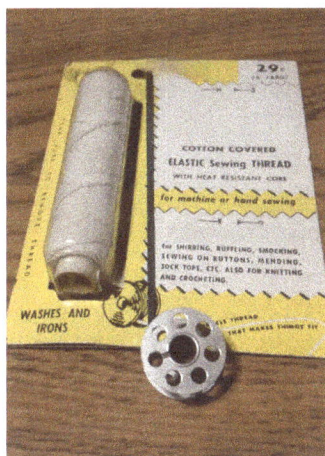

Figure 2-21   Elastic thread

Use regular thread on the top of the machine and the elastic thread on the bobbin, which gathers up the fabric as you sew.

Waistbands ————

Waistbands may have interfacing, darts, or elastic and are simple to make. There are three types of waistbands. The first type of waistbands have elastic (figures below).

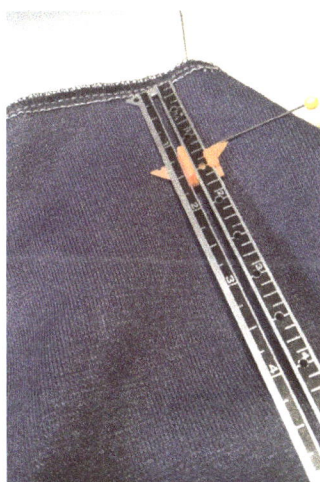

Figure 2-22

Figure 2-23

Figure 2-24

Figure 2-25

Elastic waistbands have an elastic drawstring going through a casing at the waistline (figure 2-26 and 2-27).

Figure 2-26

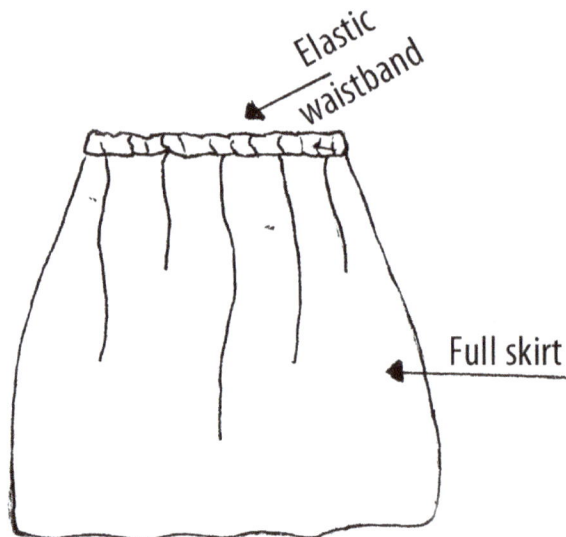

Figure 2-27

You will first sew a casing to form the waistband, and then insert elastic into the waistband sleeve (figures 2-28 and 2-29). Cut the elastic a bit longer than your waist measurement as you will need to sew the ends together after threading the elastic all the way through the casing.

Figure 2-28

Figure 2-29

To thread the elastic through the casing, attach a large safety pin to one end of the elastic (figures 2-28 and 2-29), insert the safety pin into an open end of the casing (figure 2-30), and then use your fingers from the outside of the casing to feed the safety pin through to the opening at the other end.

Figure 2-28

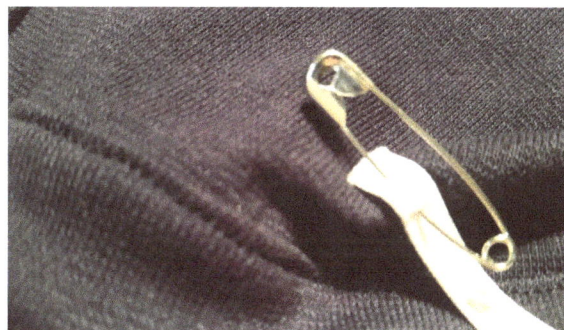

Figure 2-29

Figure 2-30

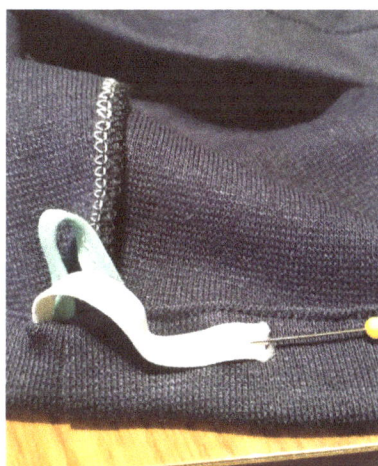

Figure 2-31

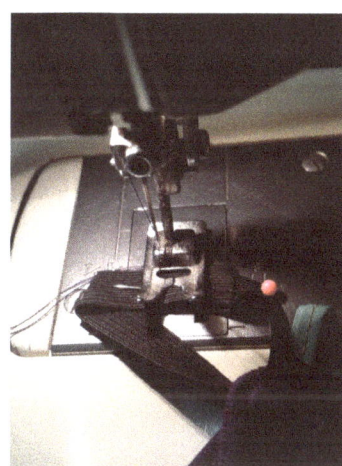

Figure 2-32

Once the end of the elastic comes out the other end of the casing, secure it with a straight pin (figure 2-31). Pull out about an inch of elastic from each end of the casing, overlap the ends, then sew them together (figures 2-32, 2-33, and 2-34).

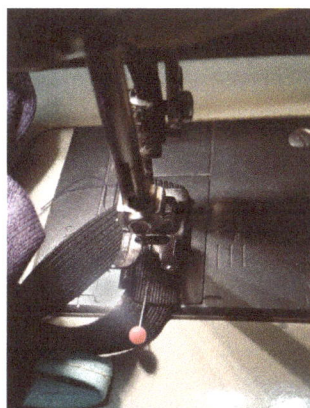

Figure 2-33

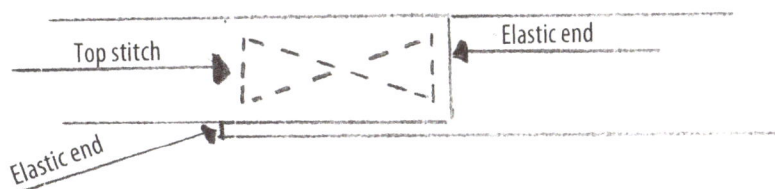

Figure 2-34

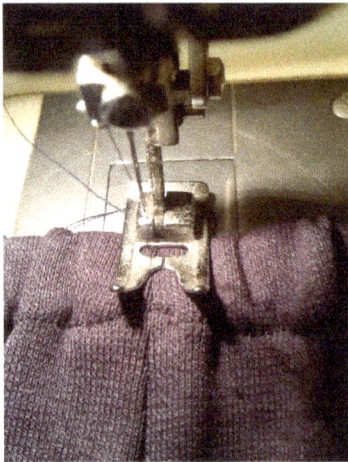

Figure 2-35

Pin a small piece of fabric (a "tag") or bias tape in the back seam to identify the back from the front of your garment (figure 2-29, pg 54). Then push the sewn together elastic ends into the opening in the casing, overlap the casing edges, and sew over the edges and through the enclosed elastic (left). This will ensure that the waistband will not roll.

The second type is hi-waisted and is tapered in at the waist and has a fabric that binds the edge on the inside of the garment (figure 2-36) like lining, will make two skirts, outside and the inside is the lining. Will have a zipper and darts.

The third type of waistband is fitted and will have a button or hook to secure it at the top (figure 2-37). May also have darts, but will have a zipper.

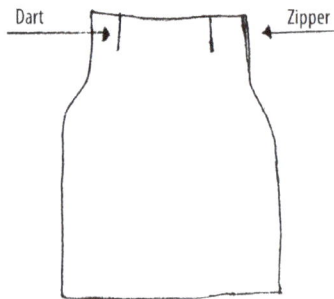

Figure 2-36

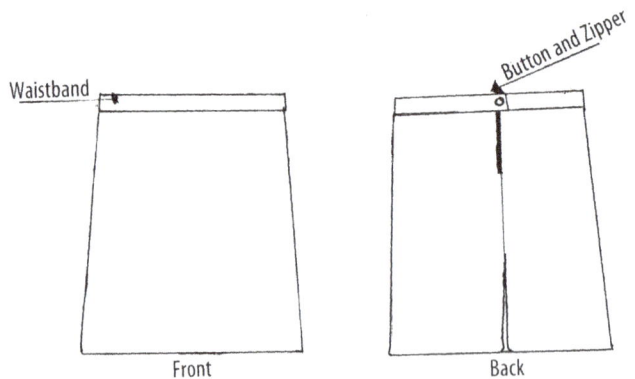

Figure 2-37

Pants and Skirts ———

Pants and skirts are probably two of the easiest garments to sew. The zipper is the most difficult part of these projects. The waistbands in this pattern's first three images are elastic, which are easy to sew (figure 2-38). Some patterns show first sewing up the sides and the inside seams, while leaving the trunk open. (figure 2-39). It is incorrect to sew an inside leg, then open up and sew the trunk in the crotch area to the back (figure 2-40). This will result in one leg being bigger than the other. The correct way to sew this area is as shown (figure 2-41).

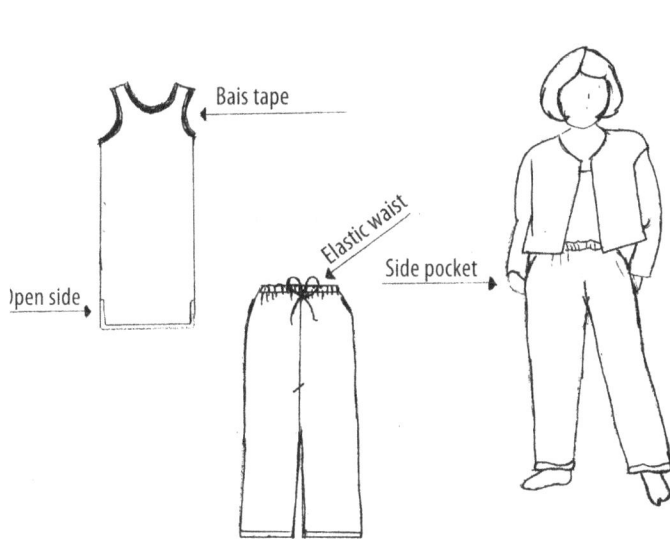

Figure 2-38

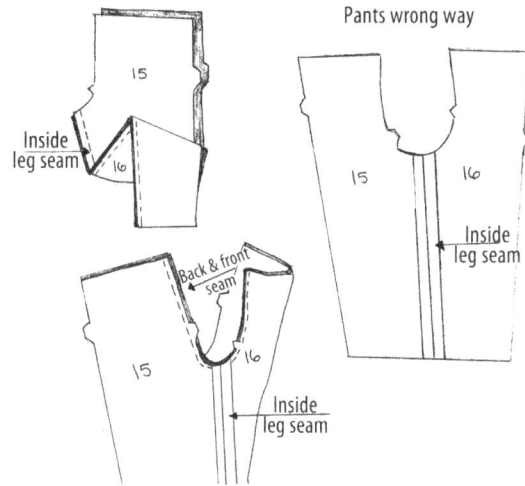

Figure 2-39

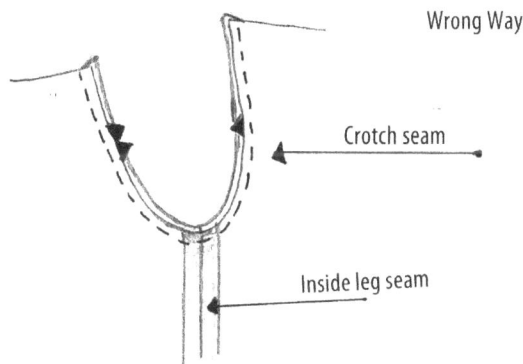

Figure 2-40

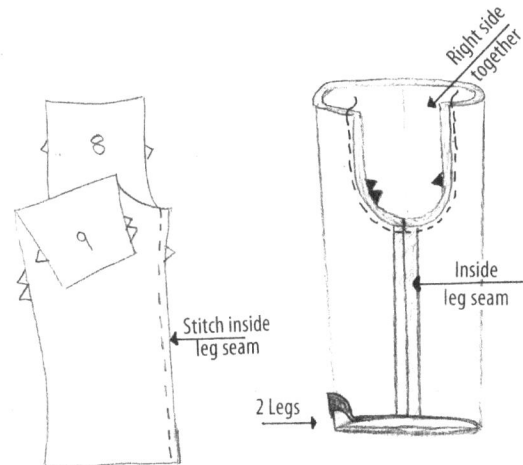

Figure 2-41

Think of a pillowcase. If you were to slide one leg into the other leg, then you can sew that whole area from the top of the front of the waistband all the way through the crotch to the back area (figure 2-240). When opened up, the garment will have two legs exactly the same size. An elastic waistband in either pants or a skirt is the easiest to sew. If the garment has a zipper, then a beginner should first practice sewing a zipper using fabric scraps as this is a more challenging skill.

Understand the layout for pants. The back piece is bigger than the front so that the pants are not too tight when you sit down. When cutting out the pattern pieces, the back will have three

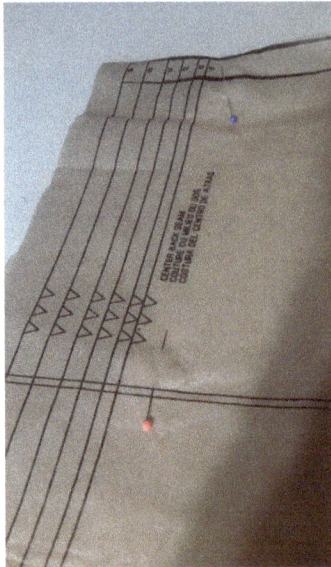

Figure 2-42

notches (figure 2-42) and the front will have two notches.

When sewing a skirt, first sew the sides together. Skirts with elastic waistbands, like pants, are the easiest to sew. Some may have pockets in a side seam (figure 2-43) or on the outside of the back. Check the pattern for instructions on pockets.

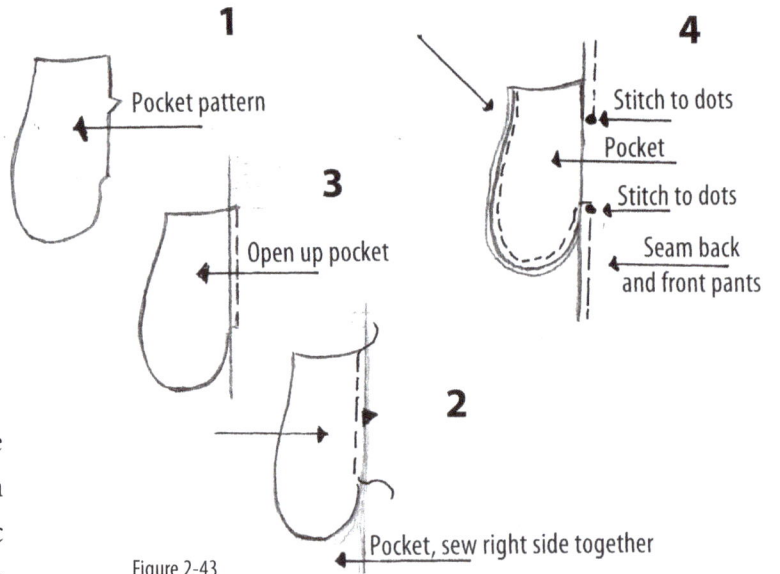

1

Pocket pattern

3

Open up pocket

2

Pocket, sew right side together

4

Stitch to dots

Pocket

Stitch to dots

Seam back and front pants

Figure 2-43

Gathering and Ruffles

Gathering is used for skirts that are full at the waistband. Gathering can also be used on sleeves to ease fabric into where the sleeve fits around the shoulder (figure 2-44). Ruffles have gathering in them. Many arts and crafts items also have gathering in them. Always use two rows of stitches (below) in case one of the threads breaks while gathering the fabric you still have one row of thread to work with.

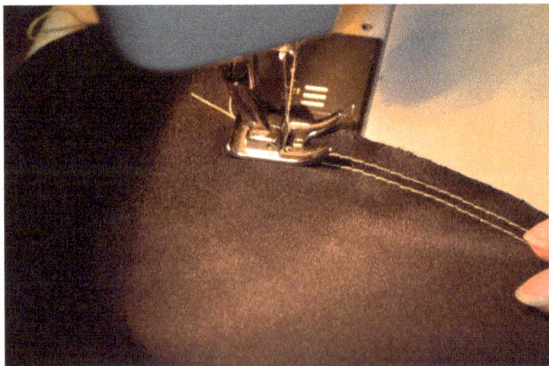

Figure 2-44

Figure 2-45

When gathering the waistband of a garment like a skirt, do not go all the way around the whole waistband with two continuous rows of stitches. This will put tension on the stitches and the thread will break. Instead, sew in sections, going from seam to seam. Start new stitching after each seam, leaving loose threads at the end of each section (figures 2-46, 2-47).

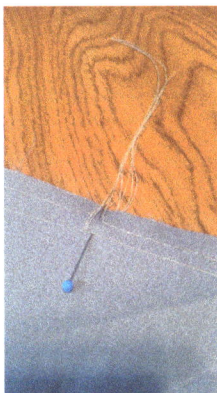

Figure 2-46 Gathering thread

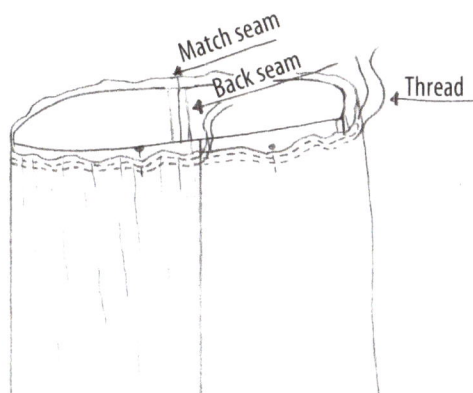

Figure 2-47

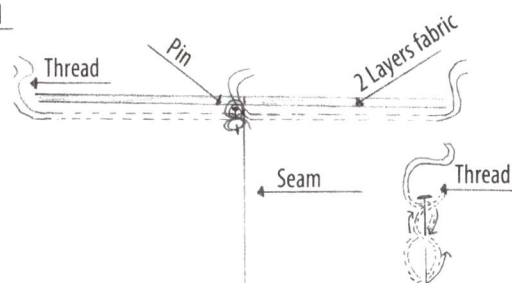

Figure 2-48

When matching up fabric at the seams (figure 2-47), put a straight pin into the garment and wrap the loose threads around it (2-48). As you are gathering the fabric, this will keep the gathered part from coming off the other end. Now secure that area by wraping the thread around the pin. Spread the fabric out with your fingernail so that area will lay flat (figure 2-49). The garment will then have a section of fabric on one side that is flat. Ease the top piece with the gathering in it to fit that flat area. When working with a sleeve, you do not want it to look puffy or see the gathering. In some skirts, the gathering will be seen. When easing in a sleeve, you want to make sure that there are two rows of stitches because it is easier to work with. First try this technique on a scrap piece of fabric for practice. By using two rows of stitching, the fabric lays flatter and it easier to sew each section.

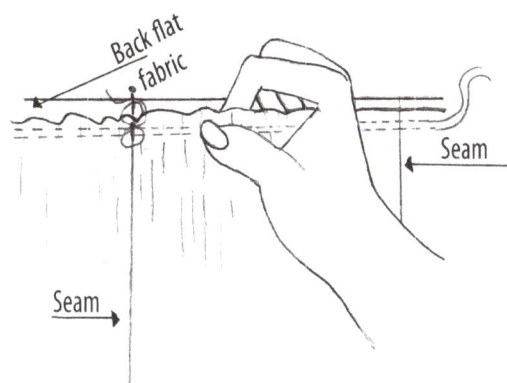

Figure 2-49

Sleeves ———————

Look back at the previous section on gathering. Now look at your sleeve. Some patterns show to first sew up the seam in the sleeve, and then sew the garment seam. When you insert and sew the sleeve, it will make a circle at the sleeve's shoulder opening (figure 2-50). The only time you would sew up the garment seam first is when making a jacket that has several pieces to the sleeve (figure 2-51).

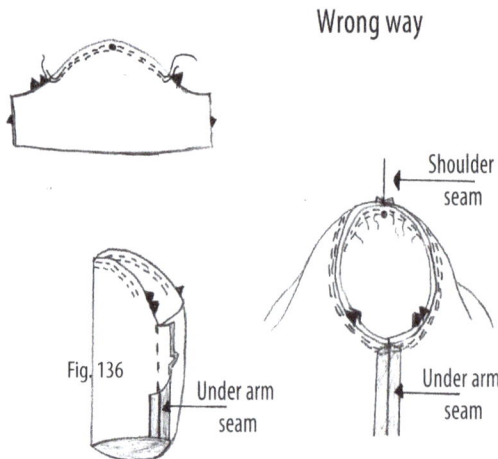

Figure 2-50

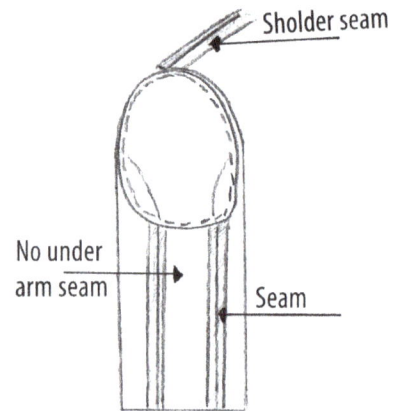

Figure 2-51

I recommend beginners choose patterns where the sleeves have only one piece. Make two rows of stitching, using a loose stitch, to gather the top of the sleeve to the shoulder (figure 2-52), then gather to fit the flat piece where the shoulder is located (figure 2-53 and 2-55).

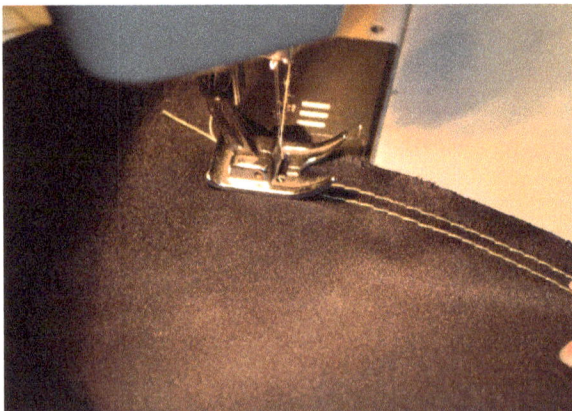

Figure 2-52 Two-row stitching

Figure 2-53

When sewing a sleeve, no matter what your pattern says, use this example for setting in your sleeves (see figure 2-54, following page). This process will make it easier to match up the seams and, if you need to adjust your garment to either let it out or take it in, it will be easier

Figure 2-54

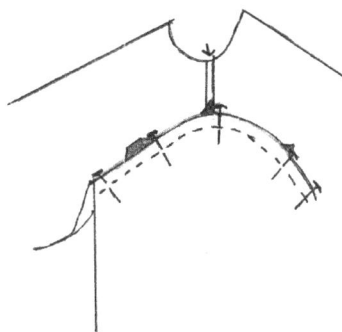

Figure 2-55

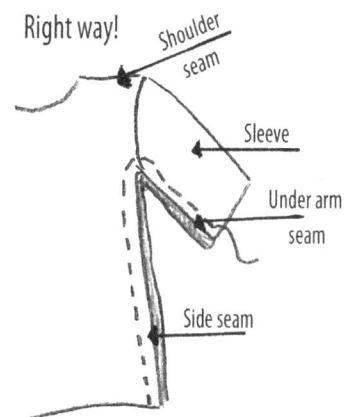

Figure 2-56

because the sleeve seam and the garment side seam go all the way around (figure 2-56). If you sew up the seam in the sleeve first, then sew the garment seam (figure 2-50, pg 60), to adjust the fit you will have to take the whole sleeve out.

Pockets ———

For an outside pocket, the pattern tissue will show a line where to place the pocket on the garment (figure 2-57). You will need to tailor tack the top two parts (figure 2-58). The pattern will not show the tailor tacking, but tailor tack as shown to mark the placement of the pocket. Finish the top edge of the pocket and turn it under, pinning it down to the garment (figure 2-59, next page). Match the pocket to the tailor tacking marks you put on the fabric once the tissue paper is off. Refer back to the Tailor Tacking section if needed.

Some garments have side pockets that are sewn into the seam of a pair of pants, a skirt, or a dress. The pattern will show a dark line on the side of the seam where these inset or hidden

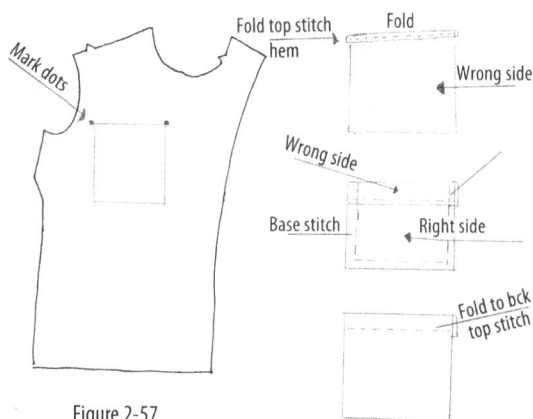

Figure 2-57

Figure 2-58

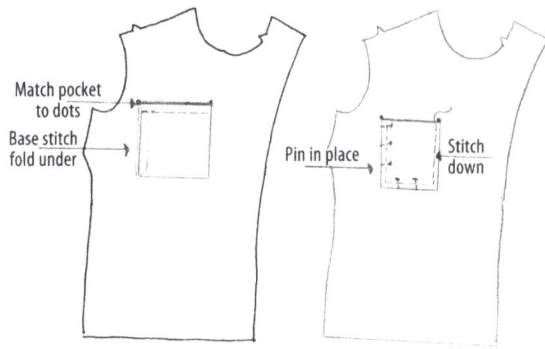

Figure 2-59

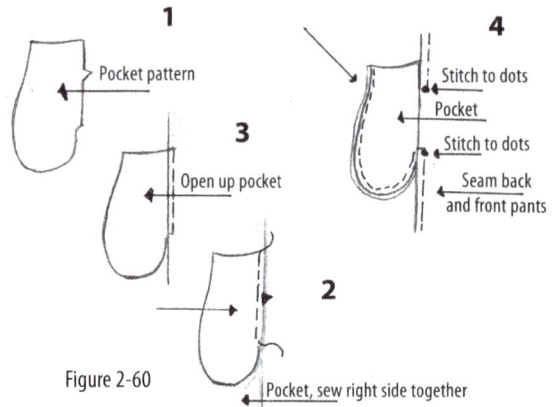

Figure 2-60

pockets will be located in the seam allowance (figure 2-59). Some garments may have both types of pockets. Jeans pockets are most often in the front or the back rather than in the seam.

Zippers

There are different types of zippers: the pink is most common as they open from the top; the white is a jacket zipper which opens from the bottom to be able to first put the jacket on, and then zip up (figure 2-61); the blue represents invisible zippers which are hidden within the seam.

Figure 2-61

The zipper foot that goes on the sewing machine to replace the presser foot looks like it has a little guide on the top part that can slide the foot over to the right or the left. Unscrew the presser foot and attach the zipper foot onto your machine (figure 2-63). A zipper is used to make it easier to get in and out of a garment. Buttons, Velcro, and hooks are also used for this purpose. While zippers are most commonly used, sewing in a zipper can be a difficult skill for beginners to master.

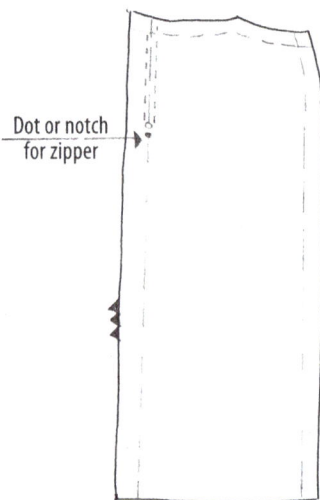

Figure 2-63

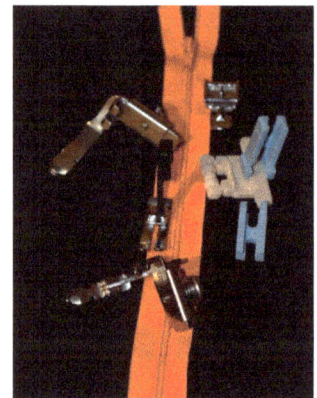

Figure 2-62

To sew in a zipper, use a basting stitch which is the loosest stitch setting on your machine (figure 2-64). First, sew down the seam that the zipper is going into with the loose stitches (figure 2-62). Sew to the small dot that shows where the zipper

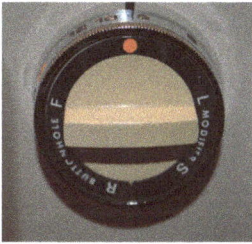

Figure 2-64 Tension stitch

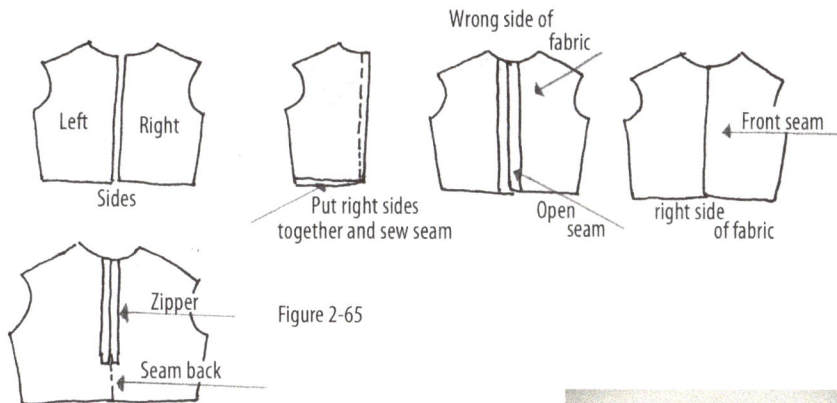

Figure 2-65

Figure 2-66

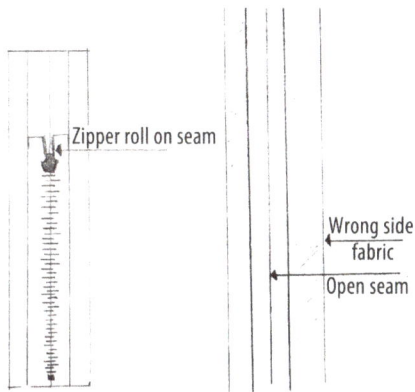

Figure 2-67

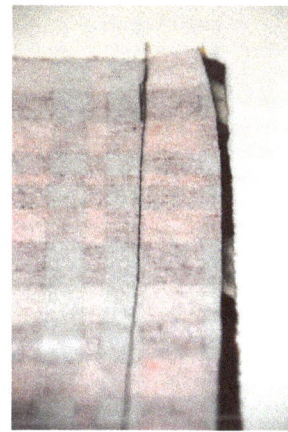

Figure 2-68

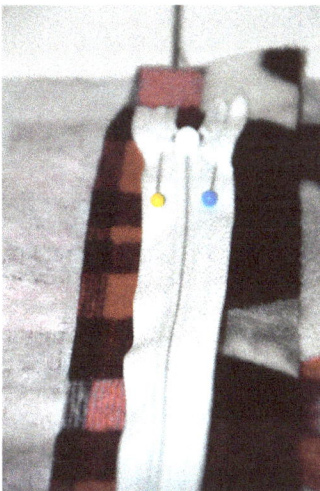

Figure 2-69

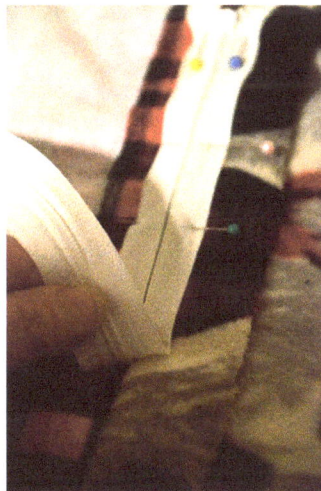

Figure 2-70

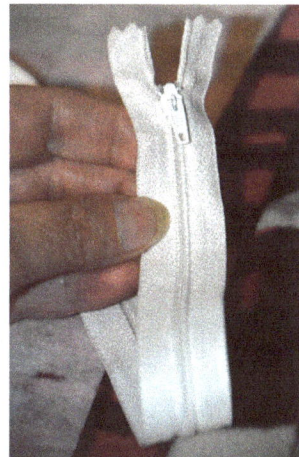

Figure 2-71

ends at the tailor tack, and then use the reverse button to backstitch (figure 2-65). Set the machine to a regular stitch and continue sewing. When done, open up that seam and either iron it or finger press it open, depending on the fabric (figures 2-66 and 2-67).

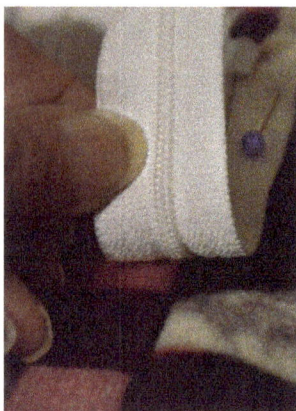

Figure 2-72

Figure 2-73

Figure 2-74

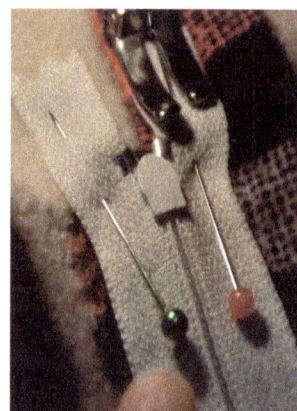

Figure 2-75

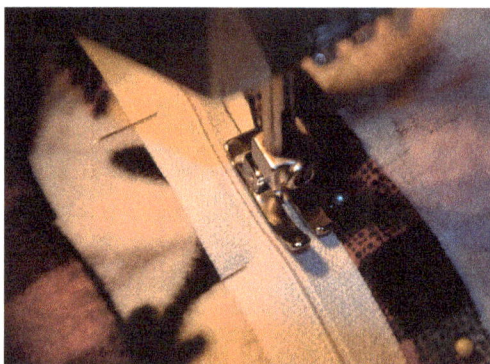

Figure 2-76

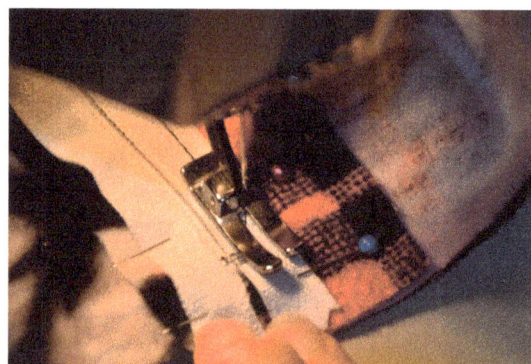

Figure 2-77

Start by taking the teeth part of the zipper (figure 2-71) and putting it teeth-side down on the wrong side of the fabric seam (figure 2-69). Unroll the zipper, aligning the teeth with the seam line and pin to secure each end at the bottom of the zipper (figure 2-69). From these anchor pins, begin pinning across the teeth, about an inch apart, moving to the top of the zipper (figure 2-70). This will hold the zipper in place, lined up with the seam, while sewing. Continue pinning all the way to the top of the zipper where the zipper pull tab is located (figure 2-73).

Some zipper feet can be moved to the right or left by loosening a screw so that you can sew as close to the teeth as you need (Figure 2-63, pg 62). Now start sewing along the right hand side of the zipper teeth (figure 2-75), stitching closely along the side of the teeth (figure 2-76). Continue sewing all the way to the end of the teeth (figure 2-77).

Now use the hand wheel to put the needle down through the fabric to keep your place at the end of the stitches just sewn. Lift the zipper foot and turn your fabric a quarter turn to sew across just below the end of the teeth to the other side (figure 2-78). After sewing across, turn your fabric

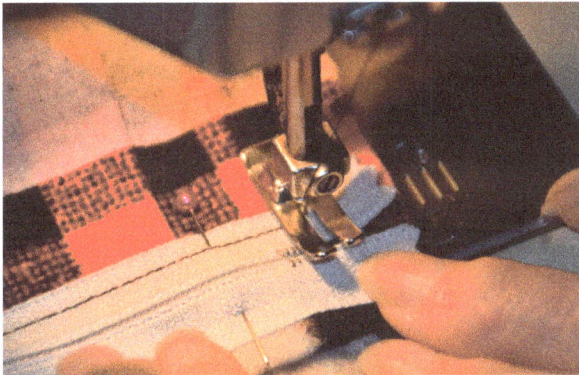

Figure 2-78

Figure 2-79

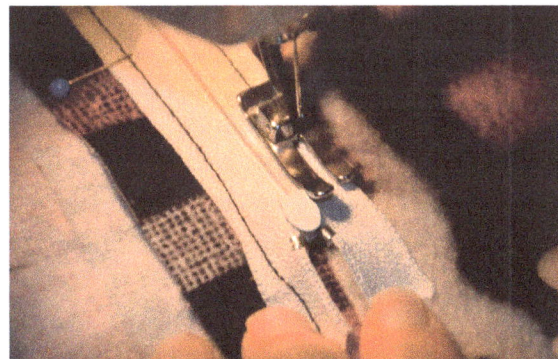

Figure 2-80

as you did before so the zipper foot is facing up the other side of the zipper (figure 2-79) and sew up to the end of that side of the zipper teeth and off the end of the zipper (figure 2-80).

Remove all the pins and turn the fabric over onto the front (figure 2-81). Using a seam ripper, open up the basting stitches (figures 2-82 and 2-83). While you can use scissors to open up the seam (figure 2-84), you will need to be very careful not to cut the fabric. The zipper is now ready to use (figure 2-85). Carefully unzip and zip the zipper a couple of times to make sure it is not catching on any of the fabric (figure2-86).

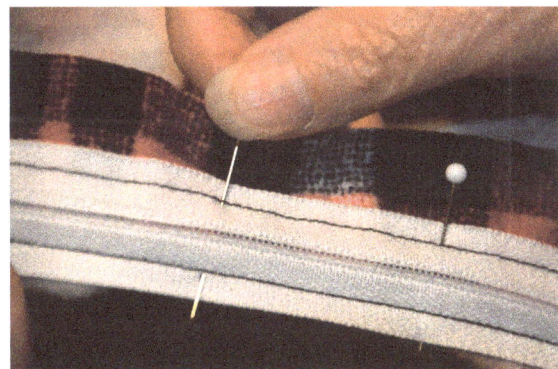

Figure 2-81

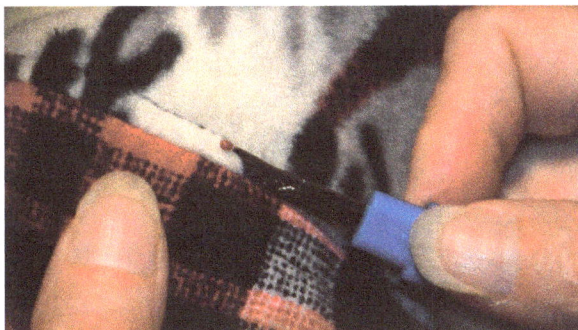

Figure 2-82

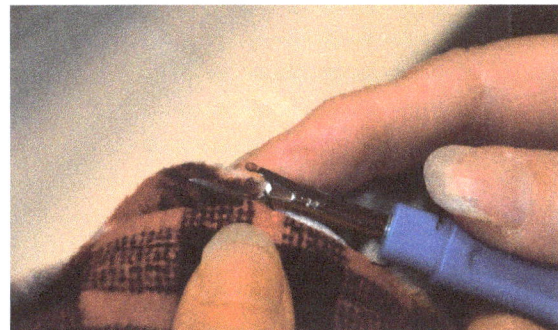

Figure 2-83

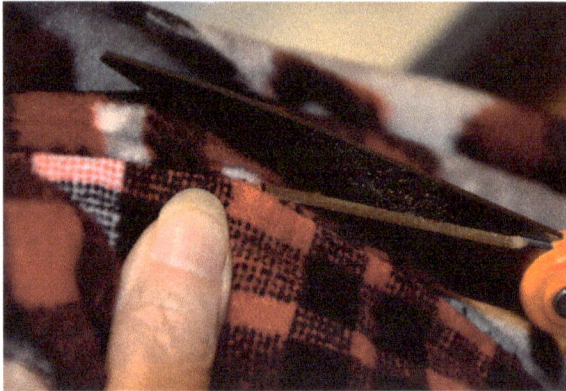

Figure 2-84

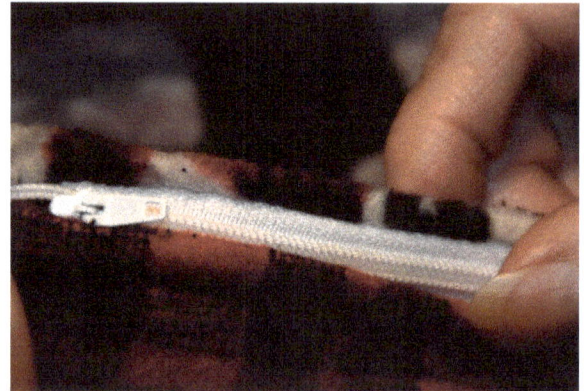

Figure 2-85

Bias Tape ───────

Bias tape is a thin piece of fabric that has been cut on an angle. It comes in many colors, widths, lace, etc. (see figure 2-87) and is found in packages, usually near the section of a fabric store where the threads are displayed. Bias tape also comes in different widths for various uses. Satin bias tape is used on the edge of a blanket. It can also be sewn around arm holes in place of interfacing. It can be used as the finishing edge of a sleeveless dress or blouse (figure 2-88).

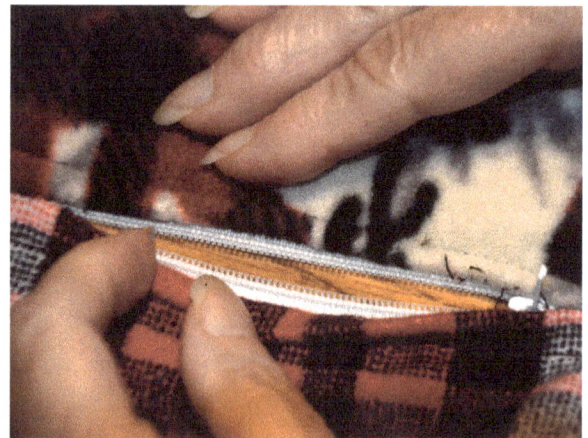

Figure 2-86

Bias tape is often used on a pillow or cushion which looks like piping. Stretch knit fabrics have bias tape along the shoulder area, which keeps the threads from breaking when the garment is stretched as it is put on and taken off. It also keeps the garment from stretching out of shape with wear. There is also flat bias tape that does not have a fold (figure 2-89) which is often used for shoulder seams. Most used bias tape has a fold in the middle and a fold on the edge to open and sew down.

Figure 2-87

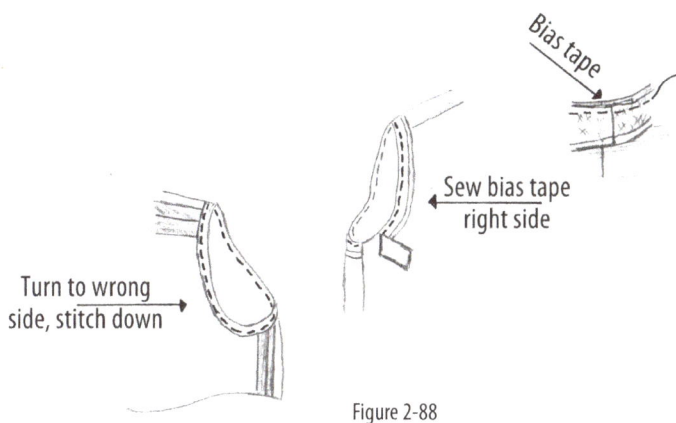

Turn to wrong side, stitch down

Bias tape

Sew bias tape right side

Figure 2-88

Figure 2-89   Bias tape, flat with no fold

Loops and Straps

Loops are very thin straps. Straps on lingerie, or spaghetti straps as they are called, are ropelike. A tool that can be purchased for more easily making loops/straps is loop turner. It is a tube with a wire that goes through it. The wire pulls the loop/strap material through the tubing within seconds rather than having to use a safety pin as was done before this tool was invented.

Author's Note
The first loop turner was invented by a man who made it for his wife. He got tired of watching her turn the loops with a safety pin, which was very time consuming.

The first step in making a loop/strap is to cut a length of the loop/strap fabric, fold it right sides together, and sew the open ends together on the long side and also sew one of the short ends together. Using the safety pin method, attach the end of one layer of the fabric to a safety pin (figure 2-90). Turn the top of the safety pin into the fabric sleeve. (figure 2-91), Then feed the safety pin through the inside of the sleeve until it comes out the other end which turns the sleeve material right side out (see figures 2-92 and 2-93).

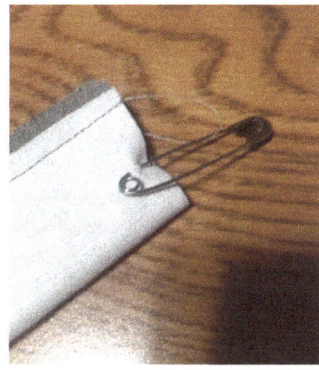

Figure 2-90

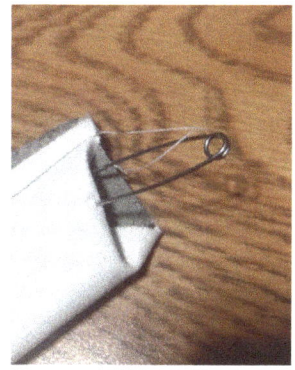

Figure 2-91

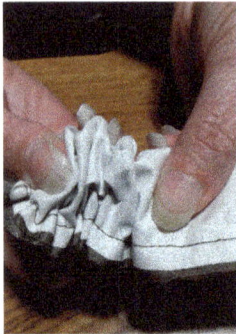

Figure 2-92

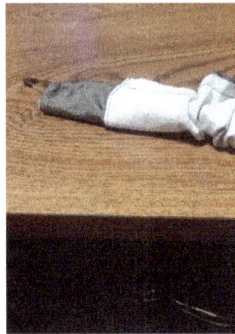

Figure 2-93

Using the loop turner, prepare the sleeve as described in the safety pin method. You will have the sleeve with one end open and the two tools that form the loop turner – the tube and the wire (see figure 2-94). Insert the tube into the open end of the sleeve (figure 2-95) and push the wire through the sleeve until it comes out at the closed end (figure 2-96).

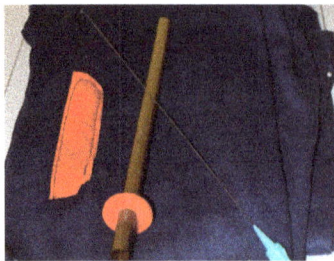

Figure 2-94

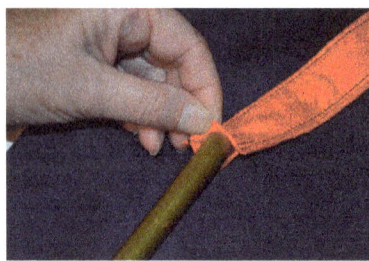

Figure 2-95

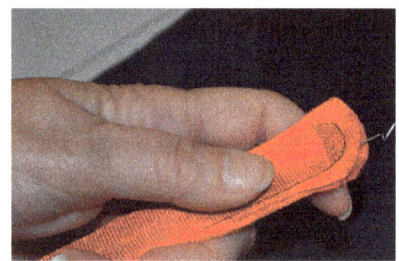

Figure 2-96

Hold the open end of the sleeve which is around the tube (figure 2-97) and then carefully pull the wire back out of the tube (figure 2-98) to turn the fabric sleeve right side out. Online, you can find a picture of a vintage loop turner and its instructions (figure 2-99).

Figure 2-97

Figure 2-98

Figure 2-99

Pleats

Pleats are often difficult for beginners to learn how to sew. Using tailor tacking can help get fabric ready to sew pleats. Pleats are made by folding the fabric and tacking it in place. Think of a paper fan. The folds of the fan are pleats. A pleat is made using two vertical lines with one line designating the fold for the pleat and the other the position that forms the pleat. Use the thread

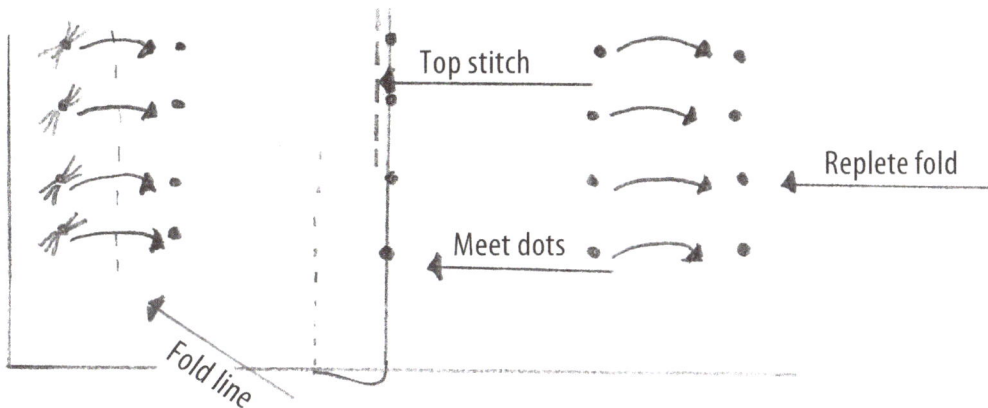

Figure 2-100

process of tailor tacking to match the dots so the fabric can be folded into pleats (figure 2-100). Then top stitch the pleat down to secure it (figures 2-101 thru 2-103).

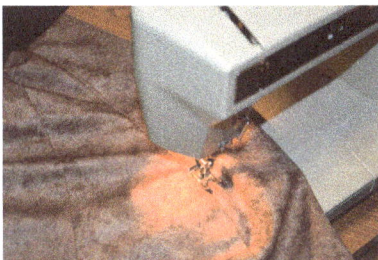

Figure 2-101

Figure 2-102

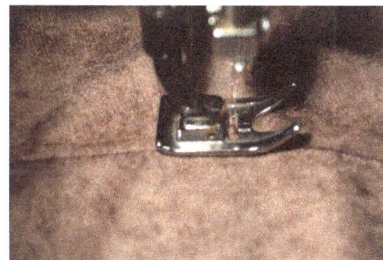

Figure 2-103

Collars and Yokes

Interfacing is always used when sewing a collar. Pin the interfacing on the wrong side of one of the two pieces of fabric. Then put the right sides of the two fabric pieces together The interfacing will now be on the outside (figure 2-104).

A yoke is a piece of fabric on a shirt, blouse, or top of a dress that provides support around the shoulders and upper back. It looks like one piece of fabric that comes down the front

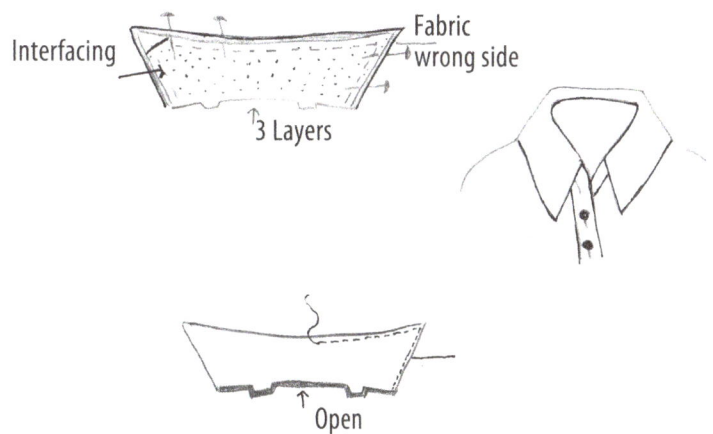

Figure 2-104

Back Yoke

Front Yoke

Back Yoke

Figure 2-105

and back of the shoulder and may or may not have a shoulder seam (figure 2-105). Some yokes have a point in the front or back. These yokes are mostly found on Western-style shirts. Sewing a garment that has a yoke is challenging for a beginner. Start with simpler patterns to build your skills and technique before trying a pattern with a yoke.

Figure 2-107   Buttonhole attachments

Buttonholes ———

Many older sewing machines have a buttonhole attachment. This has two parts: the attachment itself and a throat plate (Figure 2-106). The bottom of the attachment opens up and you will find a bar inside. This can be changed out for different size bars to make different size buttonholes. If you have the booklet for this attachment, read through how to use it and practice on separate fabric. This attachment is easy to use as the measuring is done for you. This attachment makes attractive buttonholes (Figure 2-108).

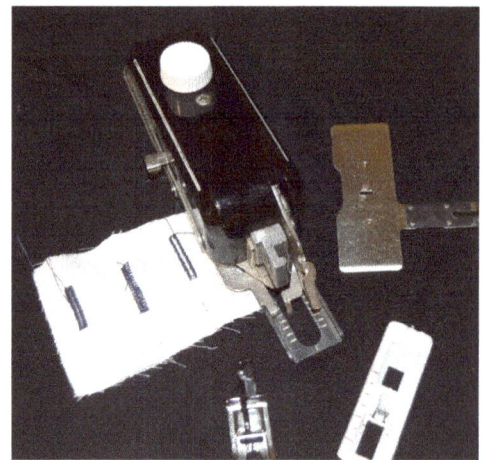

Figure 2-106 174 A Throat plate attachment

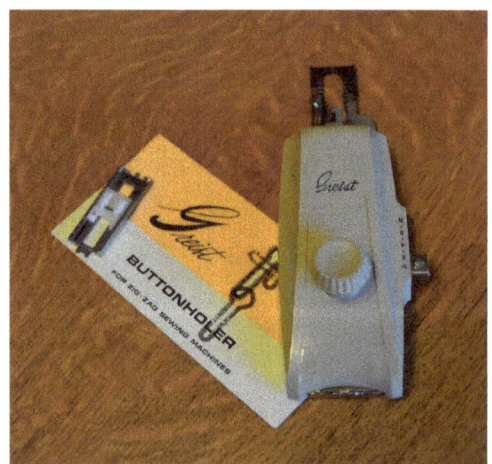

Figure 2-108   Button hole foot (Right) and Buttonhole attachment (Left)

Most machines today have just a buttonhole foot (figure 2-108). This foot attaches to the machine in place of the presser foot. Most buttonholes are rectangular in shape, with a straight both sides of the bar and a bar tack cross the top and bottom at each end. Buttonholes are not difficult to put into your fabric if using a step-by-step approach. Lay out the garment exactly as shown in the pattern, especially for a shirt. Measure the top of where the buttonhole starts and where it ends (figures 2-109, 2-110). Measure on your garment where to start the buttonhole and where it will end. Put one pin in the fabric where to start the buttonhole and another one at the end of the buttonhole (figure 2-111). Mark all buttonholes this way.

Figure 2-109

Figure 2-110

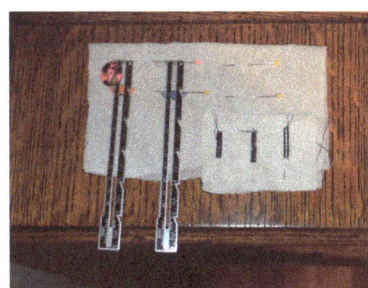
Figure 2-111

For a beginner, there are three ways to make a button hole: A buttonhole made with a Zig-Zag stitches on the machine, simply use the zigzag setting on their regular machine. Hand sewn buttonholes take a lot of time and can be hard to do or using a buttonhole attachment. Your pattern tissue will show where the buttons and buttonholes are to be placed. Only Tailor tack the buttonholes, not the placement of the buttons (figures 2-112, 2-113). Once the buttonhole is sewn, either with a machine or by hand, there will be two equal side of stitches (figures 2-114 and 2-115).

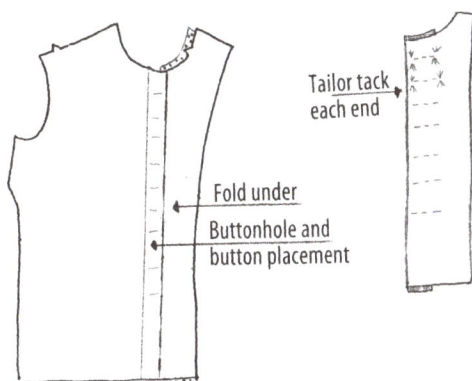

Tailor tack each end

Fold under

Buttonhole and button placement

Figure 2-112

Figure 2-113

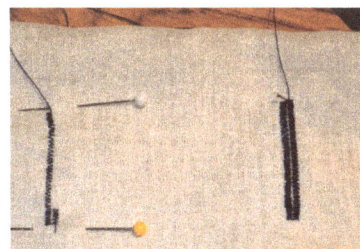
Figure 2-114

Figure 2-115

If using the sewing machine for zig zag stitching, turn the knob (figure 2-116) to the buttonhole setting. In this picture you can see the R – F. Start at the top of the buttonhole on either the right or left side. Sew down to the bottom pin. Raise the needle out of the fabric and turn the knob on the sewing machine which will make a bar-tack across the bottom of the buttonhole

 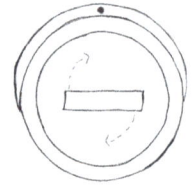

Figure 2-116   Figure 2-117   181

(figure 2-117). Turn the knob to go back up the other side, then bar-tack at the top. Repeat this process to sew over the stitches just made to make the buttonhole border stronger.

All buttonholes need to be opened once the stitching is completed (figure 2-118) This is so the button can slip through the opening and hold the garment from opening up (figure 2-119). There are two ways to make a slit in the fabric between the stitch lines. One way is to put a pin on one end of the buttonhole and then fold the buttonhole in half and clip (figure 2-120). Slowly cut it open with a

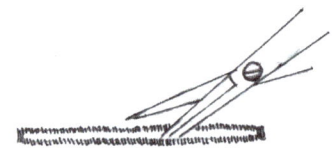

Figure 2-118

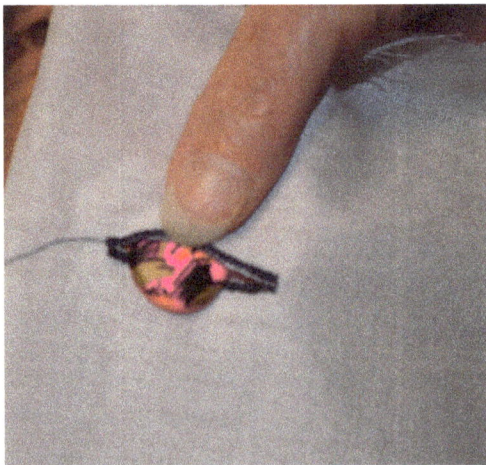

Figure 2-119

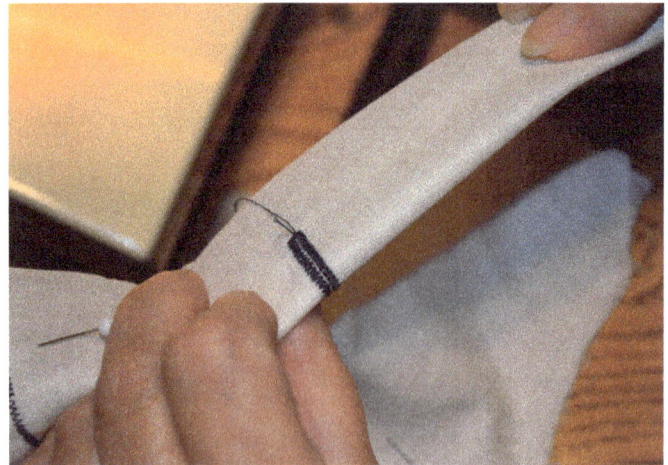

Figure 2-120

seam ripper or scissors (figure 2-121). With the scissors, slide and clip to the pin, turn the fabric around and slide and clip to the other pin (figures 2-122 and 2-123). The pins are there to stop you from cutting past the stitching.

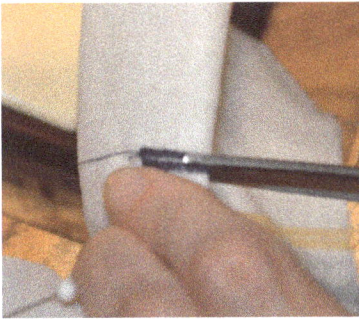

Figure 2-121 Clip

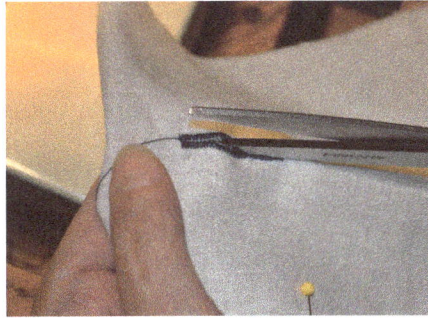

Figure 2-122

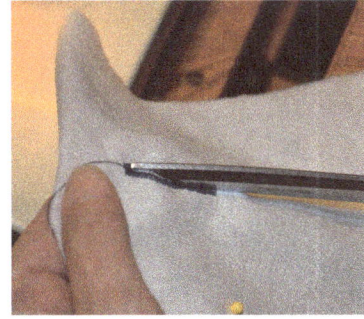

Figure 2-123 Clip

Making a buttonhole by hand takes patience as it takes much longer than using a machine. You have to first cut the buttonhole in the correct location on the fabric and then hand sew around the hole with the buttonhole stitch (figure 2-124) but very close together. The hand sewing can be done by sewing down one side, and then cut to make the opening. Turn the fabric to sew down the other side like shown here with a zipper (see figures 2-125, 2-126, and 2-127).

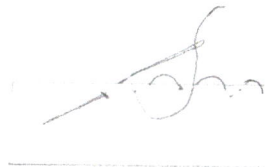

Figure 2-124 207 A

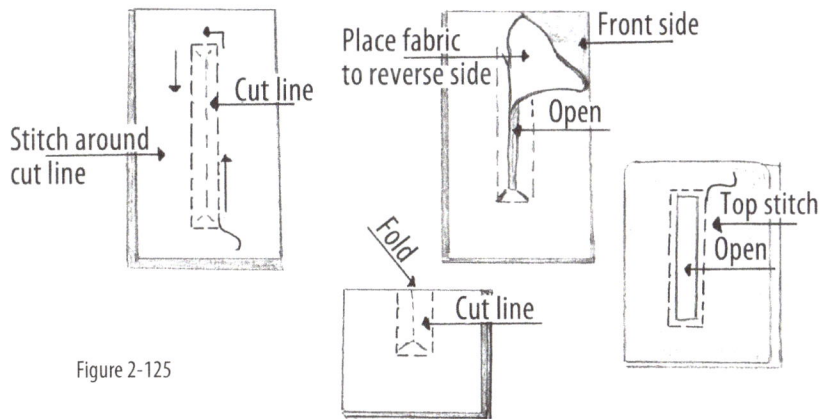

Figure 2-125

Stitch around cut line

Cut line

Place fabric to reverse side

Front side

Open

Fold

Cut line

Top stitch

Open

Figure 2-126 Needle down, foot up to turn

Figure 2-127

If you have a buttonhole attachment, refer to the booklet that shows how to use this to make a buttonhole.

Buttons and Hand Sewing ⎯⎯⎯⎯

Practice each of the steps below as shown in the pictures. Cut a length of thread and put one end through the eye of your needle, then hold the thread between your fingers (figure 2-128). Wet the top of your index finger (figure 2-129) which will make it easier to roll the thread back and forth. Move the top of your finger to make a knot (figures 2-130 and 2-131).

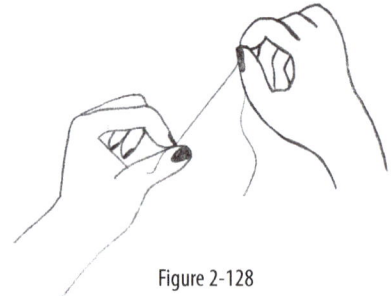

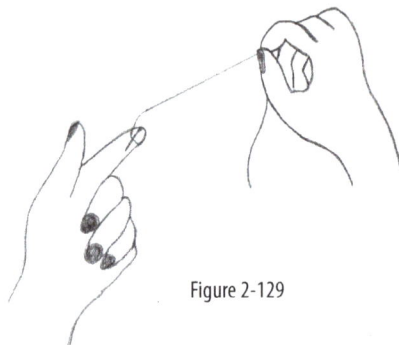

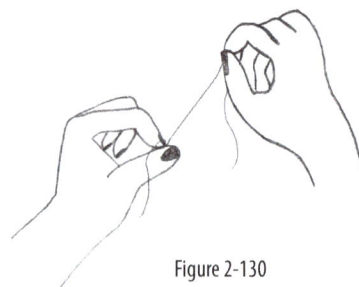

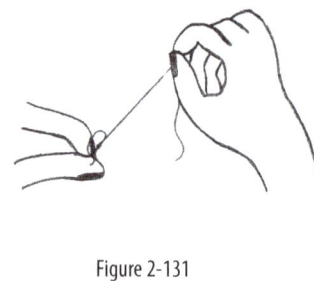

Figure 2-128

Figure 2-129

Figure 2-130

Figure 2-131

There are different threads for buttons. (figure 2-132) Top of the spool of thread is colored for the different types of thread. Cotton, Silk, Heavy Duty (used for metal buttons) and All Purpose. Sometimes a pair of pants has a metal button. Over time, that metal button (figure 2-133) starts cutting through the thread with which it was sewn. Each time the garment is worn or washed, the button cuts through the thread and eventually it will come off. This is common with metal buttons. To sew on a metal button so it will stay on the garment securely, you first need to thread the needle and make a knot at the

Figure 2-132

Figure 2-133

end (figure 2-134). On a new garment, mark the fabric where the button will go by putting pins where the buttonhole will start and end. (figure 2-135 and 2-136) The button will be in the center. Next put the needle with thread though the button (figure 2-137 and 2-138) then back through the fabric (figure 2-139), back up through the button and repeat. (figures 2-140 and 2-141) For metal buttons, you need to wrap the thread around the button (figure 2-142) then back through the fabric

Figure 2-134

to secure and tie off. Now, on the opposite side of button, then insert the needle and pull the needle through. Next put the needle through the fabric but do not pull the needle all the way

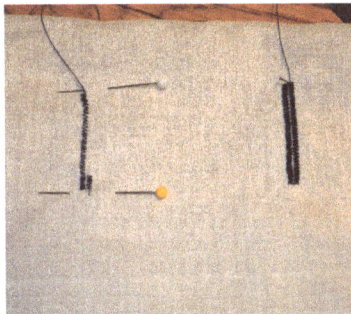

Figure 2-135

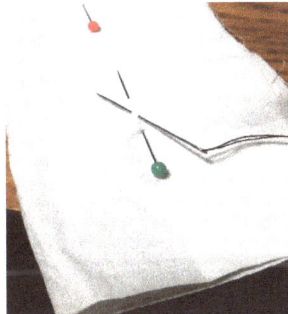

Figure 2-136

through the fabric. (figure 2-143) Now wrap the thread around the needle (figure 2-144) and pull the needle through. This will make a knot and secure the button. You can repeat the tie off. (figure 2-145) To finish, cut the thread off (figure 2-146).

Figure 2-137

Figure 2-138

Figure 2-139

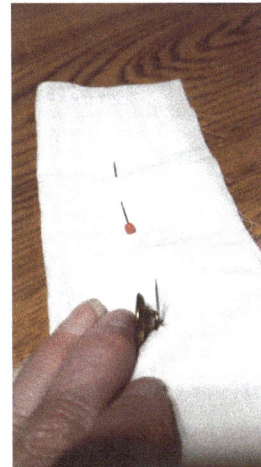

Figure 2-140

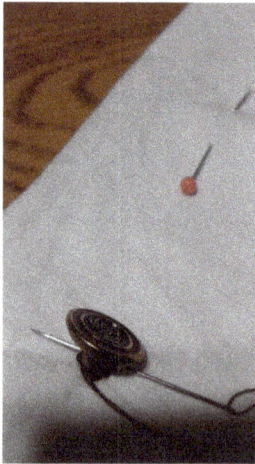

Figure 2-141

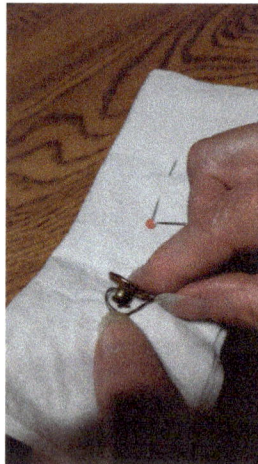

Figure 2-142

Figure 2-143

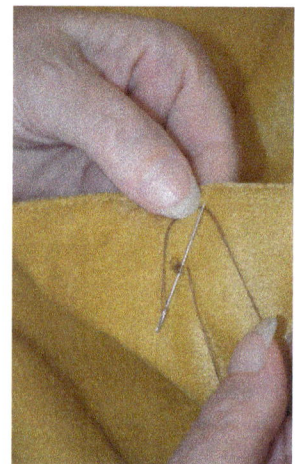

Figure 2-144

Figure 2-145

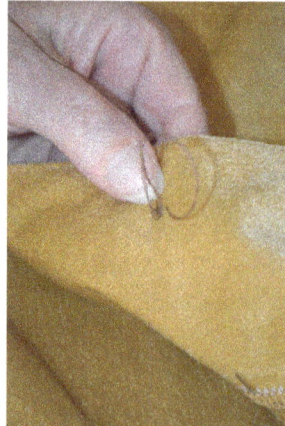

Figure 2-146

The more typical buttons have either two or four holes (figure 2-147) When attaching a button to a garment, make sure to have a secure thread with a knot at the end (figure 2-148). The knot should be on the outside of the fabric so that it will not press against the wearer's skin on the inside. Start with the knot under the front button, on the outside of the fabric (figure 2-149). Push the needle through back of button side hole to the front of the button (figure 2-147) and cross over to the second hole in the button.

Figure 2-147

Figure 2-148

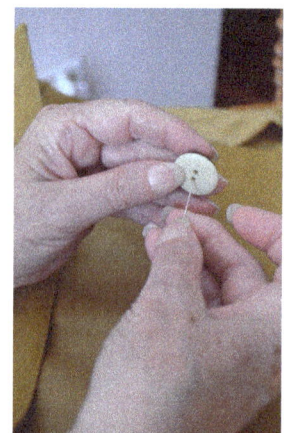

Figure 2-149

Push the needle down through the fabric (Figure 2-150) pull tight so button lays flat on fabric (figure 2-151), repeat 3 times (figure 2-152). Now tie off same as for the metal button. The buttons are all secure on the garment (figure 2-153).

Figure 2-150

Figure 2-151

Figure 2-152

Figure 2-153

With buttons and buttonholes, it is best to use interfacing or a stabilizer fabric underneath when sewing. The reason for this is so the fabric will not tear or shred away. If you ever had a shirt with a buttonhole that had frayed, it probably did not have interfacing. Buttons without interfacing may tear through the fabric and make a hole.

French Hem ———

A French hem (or seam) is totally different from a traditional dress hem. A French hem refers to a double seam that is used to hide the rough edges of fabric on the inside of a garment. These are tricky to sew, therefore not appropriate for a beginner. They are used for fabric that is very sheer. If you were to make a garment that is see-through, and you do not have a serger, then use the French hem. A French hem is just re-sewing the garment to hide the seams. When looking at the inside of the garment, there will be no raw edges of any kind (figure 2-154). Once you have become more confident with your sewing skills, French seams are not difficult if you remember that you are starting to sew the garment with the wrong sides together with a very small

Figure 2-154

seam allowance. Then you turn the garment right side out and pin it down (figure 2-155, 2-156, and 2-157). After you have sewn the original seam, then resew it a second time with a smaller seam allowance. When opened up to the inside, the raw, frayed edges will not show.

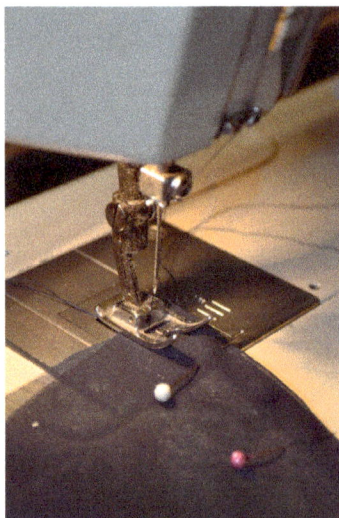

Figure 2-155

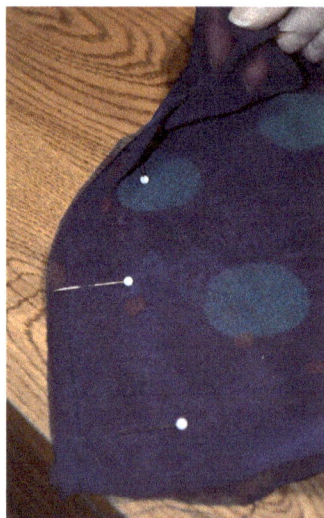

Fig.ure 2-156

Figure 2-157

When you come across something that you are sewing that calls for a French hem, it doesn't mean it is at the bottom of the garment. It means that every seam that will be sewn will be hidden. Usually, the fabric will be very lightweight or very sheer, so you do not want the seams to show through from the outside. For much of the time you will be sewing the garment inside out, and then turning each seam over and stitching it down so that the seam is completely hidden (figure 2-158). While difficult to master this technique, it produces a very delicate look to your finished garment (figure 2-159). If you want to attempt this, I recommend you practice several of these hidden seams on extra, sheer fabric pieces before attempting a full garment.

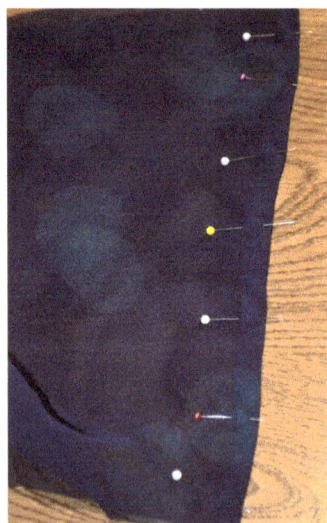

Figure 2-158

Figure 2-159

Hemming————

A hem is made to provide a finished edge at the bottom of a garment. The hem secures an edge of the fabric so it does not have a raw (unfinished) edge and also so that it will not unravel. One type of hem is a rolled hem, which is made by a sewing machine. If using a knit fabric, two rows of stitches must be sewn (figure 2-160) to prevent stitches from breaking when the fabric is stretched.

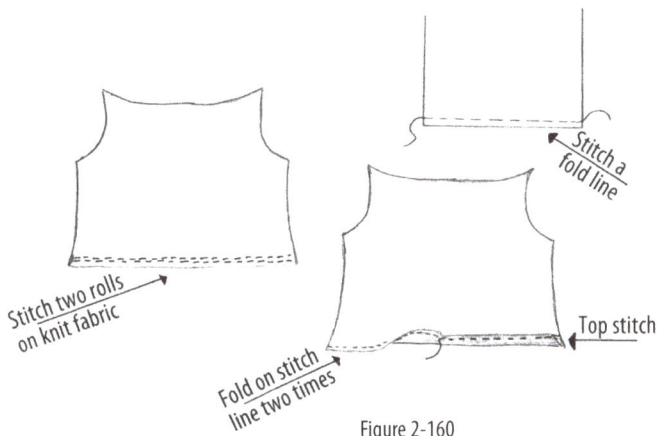

Figure 2-160

If making a hem on a nice pair of wool pants, dress pants, or fabric that is bulky, use hem bias tape (figure 2-161). The bias tape to use will say, "For hemming." It is a flat, silky-looking fabric or it looks like lace, and comes in packages found in the area where threads are displayed in a fabric store. Sew the hem tape to the edge of the fabric, measure the width of the hem to turn up from the outside to the inside. Then hand stitch the hem in place at the edge of the bias tape on the inside of the fabric.

My favorite hand stitch is one that interlocks the stitches. It looks like a Lock Stitch (figure 2-162) Cross stitch when sewing it (figure 2-163, 2-164).

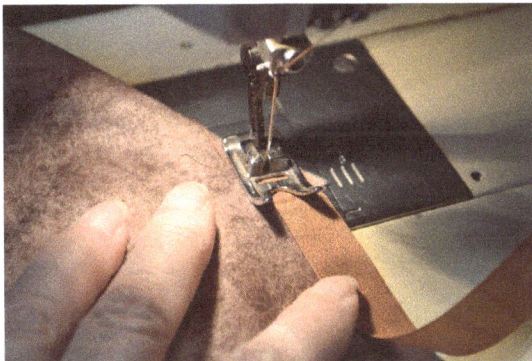

Figure 2-161

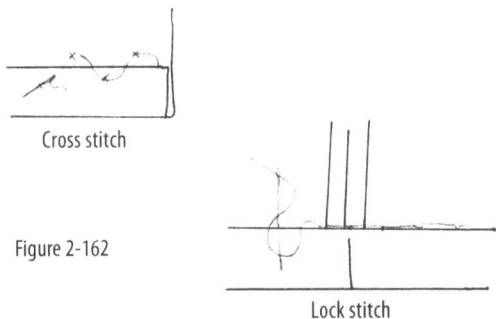

Cross stitch

Figure 2-162

Lock stitch

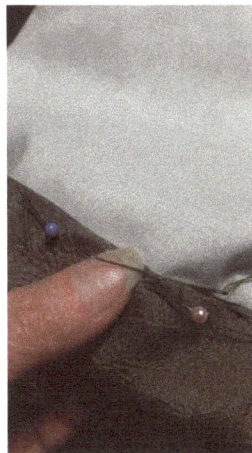

Figure 2-163

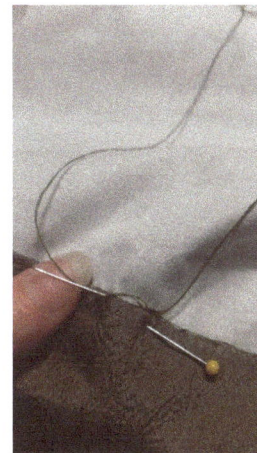

Figure 2-164

This stitch will not show very much on the outside of your fabric if sewn correctly. If the hem catches and breaks some threads, with this lock stitch the hem will not unravel as each stitch is locked with the next stitch. If enough hem stitching breaks, and the hem drops down at the bottom of the garment, a temporary fix can be made using scotch tape or staples. Using the interlocking stitch will prevent this from happening.

The other hem is the rolled hem. You want to make sure when measuring, the rolls are of different lengths (figure 2-160 pg. 79) If shortening a garment 4 inches, do not cut the fabric off at 4 inches as an extra 2 inches are needed to roll up the hem and sew it down. This is for jeans and skirts. When looking at the garment you are going to hem up shorter, if you see that it already has stitching on it, then it is machine stitched. Knitted fabrics require sewing two rows of stitches so it doesn't roll while wearing it. Practice these stitches on scrap pieces of fabric before starting to hem the garment.

Hand Sewing and Hemming ———

For hand sewing you need thread and a needle (figure 2-165). This information is also in Section 27 Buttons.

When hemming a garment, here are the different stitches you can use:

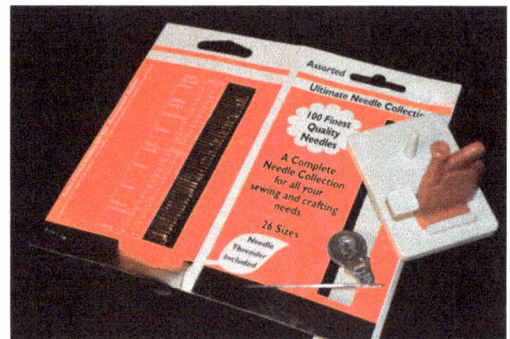

Figure 2-165

Running Stitch – This is the same as a basting stitch. Begin working from your right to the left. Weave the needle point in and out of the fabric several times before pulling the fabric off the needle (figures 2-166, 2-167).

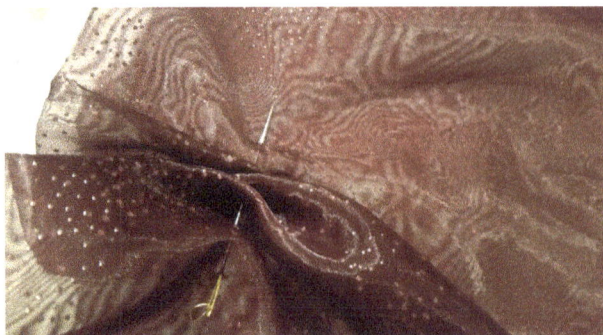

Figure 2-166

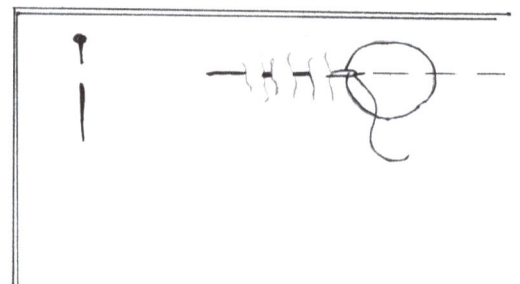

Figure 2-167

Slip Stitch – This is a fast way to hem but it can come out early if the thread gets caught and breaks. This stitch is like a running stitch, but do not gather the fabric on the needle (figure 2-168).

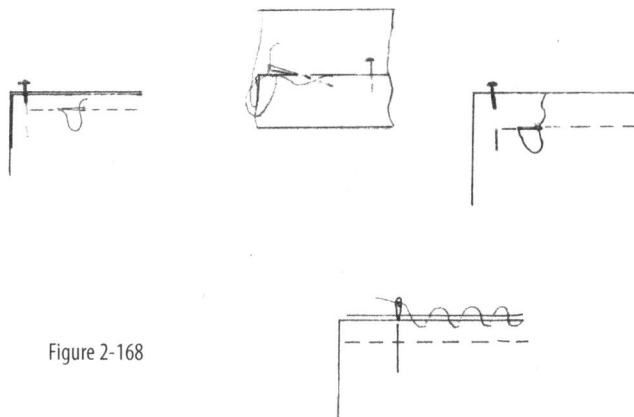

Figure 2-168

Whipping or Overcast Stitch –You can use this stitch to close up an opening like on a pillow (fig. 2-168).

Blind Stitch – This is the same as an overcast stitch. The difference is that your fabric is set up for a hem. You will take the needle into the back piece of fabric (little stitch) and come back under the hem fold to the front, then repeat (figure 2-169).

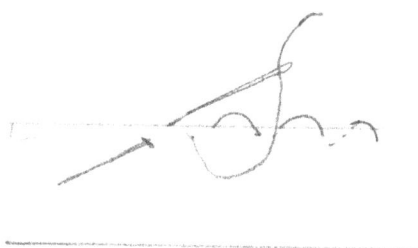

Figure 2-169

Lock Stitch – This stitch is used to lock each stitch on a hem. Start the needle under the fold of the hem to hide the knot. Take the needle and pick up the fabric knot where the fold is and then come under the fold to the front of the fold hem. Do not pull the needle all the way through. You will need to loop the thread under the needle, then pull it through the fabric, then repeat (figure 2-170).

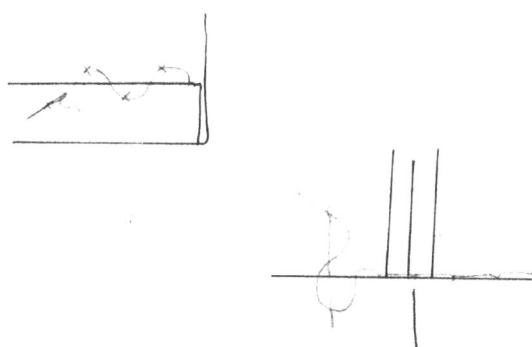

Figure 2-170

Cross Stitch – This stitch is for hemming a heavier fabric. Start stitching from right to left by taking the needle under the fold. Then take the needle to the top of the unfolded part of the hem. Pick up a small amount of fabric, then come down to the fold of the hem. Back up by moving to the left and repeat. This will look like a cross stitch (Figure 2-170).

Tailoring ———

Tailoring is not for a beginner. Tailoring requires knowledge about fabrics and experience with underlining and interfacing.

If you measure bigger on the top than on the bottom, because one leg is longer than the other, etc., you can tailor (modify) the pattern to your size. Go back to the pattern layout for shortening and lengthening (figures 2-171 and 2-172). If the pattern needs to be let out or taken in, look for a pattern that has a large seam allowance as shown in this picture (figure 2-173). Having more seam fabric to work with will make tailoring easier.

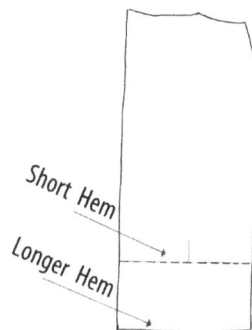

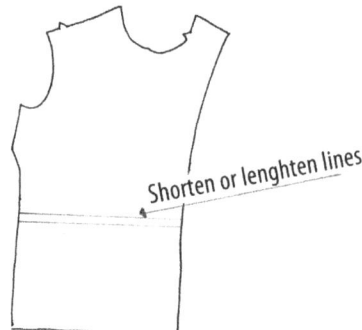

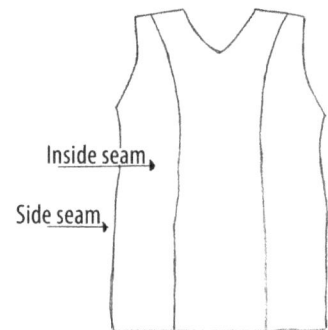

Figure 2-171   Figure 2-172   Figure 2-173

As a beginner, you won't be tailoring right away. However, this skill is a simple way to alter a pattern to fit your size. When you have made a garment that doesn't fit right, turn the garment inside out and put it on. Then pin where it needs to be taken in or let out. It is like working on a mannequin. If you put the garment on a mannequin, you can easily pin darts or waistband a little tighter on the outside of the fabric. You can then remove the garment and fix the problem areas. This is the best way to tailor a garment.

Sewing with Glued-on Sequin Fabric – Follow these steps to sew on sequin fabric:

1. Make all alterations and fitting adjustments on the pattern and fabric.
2. Use a size 12 needle in your sewing machine.
3. Placing a small drop of "Sewer Aid"(can find in store) on the bottom of the presser foot and the needle will make it easier to sew this type of fabric.

4. Avoid top stitching as it will not look good on this type of fabric.

5. Sew at a very slow speed so the machine will not get too warm or create a buildup on the needle.

6. If a buildup occurs, use nail polish remover or alcohol to wipe off the needle periodically.

Measurement Chart for Bedding

Mattress Sizes

Twin	39" x 75"
Full	54" x 75"
Queen	60" x 80"
King	76"x 80"
California King	72" x 84"
Day Bed	39" x 75"
Crib	27" x 52"

Bedspread Sizes

Twin	81" x 110"
Full	96" x 110"
Queen	102" x 115"
King	120" x 115"
California King	120" x 115"

Comforter Sizes

Twin	69" x 90"
Full	84" x 90"
Queen	90" x 95"
King	106" x 98"

ACKNOWLEDGMENTS

This book has been a long time in the making, first in my head, then on paper. Having never written a book before, I had no concept of the methodology or procedure required. Simply put, "I didn't have a clue." Enter Heather Griffith. Heather transcribed from tape to paper for me, and that's what got me started. That was the beginning.

Another valued force in this effort, Donna Payne. Donna edited all my notes. That greatly helped me to continue forward.

Gayle Krzemien added much needed polish to my final manuscript, this is something she is very good at. A good fit, and knowing me well, Gayle edited with an understanding of my viewpoint.

Three good friends to my rescue, thank you Ladies for helping me make this book a reality.

www.ingramcontent.com/pod-product-compliance
Lightning Source LLC
Chambersburg PA
CBHW061417090426

42742CB00026B/3496